AMERICAN GENIUS

HENRY WADSWORTH LONGFELLOW

★★★

Books by Marian R. Carlson

John Adams: The Voice Heard 'Round the World
with companion CD narrated by David McCullough
music composed by Anthony DiLorenzo,
played by the Boston Landmarks Orchestra

Winner of a Parents' Choice Gold Award and
New England Book Show, Best in Category Elem-High School

In Search of the Great American Writers:
An Imaginary Journey Back in Time with Intrepid Reporter Nellie Bly
Phillis Wheatley, Washington Irving, Henry Longfellow,
Emily Dickinson, Louisa May Alcott, Mark Twain, Nellie Bly

Yankee Doodle's Pen: Wheatley, Washington, Longfellow

American Genius: Henry Wadsworth Longfellow

To order books or the CD, contact

Schoolmaster Press
993 Memorial Drive, Suite 101
Cambridge, MA 02138
(617) 513-9154
www.schoolmasterpress.com

AMERICAN GENIUS

HENRY WADSWORTH LONGFELLOW

A folk art depiction of Paul Revere's ride

Marian R. Carlson and Libby Hughes

Schoolmaster Press
Cambridge, Massachusetts

American Genius
Henry Wadsworth Longfellow

Schoolmaster Press
993 Memorial Drive, Suite 101
Cambridge, MA 02138
www.SchoolmasterPress.com
(617) 513-9154

The views expressed in this work are solely those of the authors and
do not necessarily reflect the views of the publisher, and the publisher
hereby disclaims any responsibility for them.

ISBN-13: 978-0-984-47763-0 (pbk)
ISBN-13: 978-0-595-86228-3 (ebk)
ISBN-10: 0-984-47763-2 (pbk)
ISBN-10: 0-595-86228-4 (ebk)

Printed in the United States of America

For Paul, Emma, Charlotte, and Elise, fifth generation
bookworms

(MRC)

For Amanda Jones, a budding poet

(LH)

Contents

Acknowledgments

With heartfelt gratitude to the Longfellow National Historic Site (Paul Blandford, Anita Israel), Maine Historical Society (Richard D'Abate, Gabrielle Daniello), Charles Calhoun, Judy Carlson, Julie Carlson, Cathy Cote, Deborah Enright, Jocelyn Hayes, Dale Myers, Kathy Petersen, Marilyn Richardson, Janet Scinto, Ben Sloan, Joan F. Smutny, and many others.

Introduction

Why do the works of certain authors, playwrights, and poets survive through the centuries?

Because they write about universal themes and about the best and worst aspects of human nature.

For those very reasons, Shakespeare has lasted for over four centuries and Henry Wadsworth Longfellow for nearly two centuries.

Why should anyone be interested in Longfellow's poetry today? It speaks to the human soul (*A Psalm of Life*) and to social and historic matters such as the plight of Native Americans (*The Song of Hiawatha*) and slavery of African Americans (*The Slave's Dream*).

Although Longfellow was a world traveler who exposed his readers to other countries and cultures, he was an American patriot at heart. His poetry sang about people (*The Village Blacksmith* and *The Courtship of Miles Standish*) and places (*Tales of a Wayside Inn*) in America. Within his verses, Americans found their national pride and identity.

Some writers use a literary device to focus public attention on certain issues. Playwright Arthur Miller did this with his 1953 play *The Crucible*, which dramatized the Salem witchcraft trials in 1692. The true purpose of the play was to parallel those events with Senator Joseph P.

McCarthy's ruthless attacks on some innocent actors and directors in Hollywood for allegedly being communists, as well as his unfounded criticism of certain government and military officials.

Henry Longfellow also used a poetic device to make a statement. In *Paul Revere's Ride*, he showed how one man in war, or in any situation, can make a difference.

During the Civil War, President Abraham Lincoln found great comfort in Longfellow's poem *The Building of the Ship*. He wept openly because the verses about union, faith, and triumph encouraged him. The poem was written in 1849, but Lincoln read it in the 1860s at the height of the tumult between the States.

Longfellow fans were from all over the world. They ranged from servants and farmers to kings and queens. Many of them could quote his poems from memory. Even today Senator Edward M. Kennedy of Massachusetts and Senator Robert C. Byrd of West Virginia are among those who can repeat *Paul Revere's Ride* by heart.

Incidentally, his meter and rhyme were forerunners to hip hop and rap music. Try putting a few Longfellow poems into rap. It works! Music and math are intertwined. Even Mozart and Bach composed masterpieces with mathematical measures. Longfellow's skill at math guided him through the rhythm of his poetry.

Longfellow, considered a bestselling superstar of his time, is the ONLY American to have his bust in Poets' Corner at Westminster Abbey in London. Yet, for all his fame, he was happiest at home with his family and friends.

The life story of Longfellow is a compelling one. He grew up in a small seaport village in Maine. There, he began to dream of wonders across the vast ocean. By working very hard, he achieved his dreams in an unlikely profession. His life brought him acclaim in the highest circles of society. Along with great success, he experienced great loss. In spite of these tragedies, he was able to get beyond personal despair to write some of his most inspired work.

It is the intention of the authors to help restore Longfellow to superstar status. *American Genius: Henry Wadsworth Longfellow* is not only for young readers, but for others who want to get a glimpse of the life of a poetic genius.

> Marian R. Carlson
> Libby Hughes
> Cambridge, Massachusetts
> 2006

CHAPTER ONE

"Listen my children, and you shall hear"

Adventurous Grandparents and Parents

1. Peleg Wadsworth, Revolutionary War general,
Longfellow's maternal grandfather

Cannons thundered. Fires flashed across the open sky. Smoke spiraled into the air. The year was 1813, and outside the Portland, Maine, harbor near Monhegan Island, a terrible sea battle was waging between the American brig *Enterprise* and the British brig *Boxer*.

The residents of Portland were terrified because they remembered how the British bombarded and burned Portland during the Revolutionary War in 1775.

Would it happen again?

After 45 minutes of fireworks, the American ship captured the British brig and towed it into port. But the death toll of both young captains was sad. At the age of six, Henry Wadsworth Longfellow watched the funeral procession go past him and the First Parish Church. He saw the captains buried side by side at the Eastern Cemetery on a hill above the inlet shores of Casco Bay.

The seaport of Portland in the early 1800s had a certain charm. It was a three and a half mile peninsula, jutting its thumb into the bay waters. During Henry's childhood, Portland remained an active city by the sea. However, President Jefferson's Embargo Act in 1807 slowed maritime commerce in Portland, throwing many exporters of lumber and fish into bankruptcy. Not until 1832 did Portland recover and prosper once again. For Henry, his house on Congress Street was at the center of everything. Congress Street was on a hill like a camel's hump. Slopes dipped to the bay on either side of the ridge. Near Henry's house was the triangular Haymarket Square where fresh fruits and vegetables were sold. There were other little shops, many churches, and the courthouse outside his front door. The harbor and wharves were only blocks away.

In fact, history and patriotism were living subjects to Henry. His grandfather Peleg Wadsworth spun many tales about the 1775 destruction of Portland (then called Falmouth). British Captain Henry Mowatt fired his cannons on the town, destroying almost 500 buildings and separating frightened families.

As a boy, Henry Wadsworth Longfellow tried not to play favorites with his grandparents. His two grandfathers were giant role models. Stephen Longfellow, his paternal grandfather, had a farm in Gorham, Maine, not too far from Portland. It was always fun to visit there and play at the farm during the summers. A Harvard College graduate, his grandfather played a major part in founding Bowdoin College (Henry's alma mater) in Brunswick, Maine.

But it was his grandfather Peleg Wadsworth, his maternal grandfather, who really captured his heart and imagination. Peleg (an old-fashioned New England name) came from Pilgrim relatives in Duxbury, Massachusetts, and was a direct descendant of Priscilla and John Alden. (Later Henry would immortalize the Puritan saga of the Aldens in the poem titled *The Courtship of Miles Standish*).

In his elder years, Peleg was an eccentric. He had been a famous general during the American Revolutionary War. He always wore a black three-cornered hat, powdered wig, knickers, white stockings, and black shoes with silver buckles. Many of Henry's young friends made fun of Peleg and laughed at him, covering their mouths with their hands, while the General strode through the Portland streets, ready to wield his walking cane if necessary.

Henry didn't care. He loved this man who bounced him on his knee as a baby and sang songs to him. He could sit at his feet for hours hearing about his war adventures and famous people in history.

Most of all, he loved walking with Peleg to the end of the Portland peninsula, overlooking the restless waters of Casco Bay and the wide Atlantic beyond. Very often they would stand in silence, gazing up and down the expanse of water. Henry would slip his hand into the cup of his grandfather's fist so that the wind wouldn't sweep him into the swallowing waves.

When waves would creep to the edge of the embankment, they would crash in an angry roar, throwing the white foam into the air and spraying the two figures—one stout and medium-tall, the other slight and small—with a soft shower of salted tears that fell in ribbons down their faces. Henry would wait and lick the salt with his tongue across his lips. Peleg did not move a muscle, but held his grandson's hand tightly in his.

As the waves were sucked back into the ebb tide, the rocks would be shiny wet and gleam in the sun. They were smooth and worn by centuries of pounding. Seaweed would be ripped from the sands beneath and rest on the surface, wandering at the whim of the waves.

Longfellow's seaside experiences are reflected in his creative work. As an example, here are three verses from his short poem called *The Tide Rises, the Tide Falls:*

> *The tide rises, the tide falls,*
> *The twilight darkens, the curlew calls;*
> *Along the sea-sands damp and brown*
> *The traveller hastens toward the town,*
> > *And the tide rises, the tide falls.*
>
> *Darkness settles on roofs and walls,*
> *But the sea, the sea, in the darkness calls;*
> *The little waves, with their soft, white hands,*
> *Efface the footprints in the sands,*
> > *And the tide rises, the tide falls.*
>
> *The morning breaks; the steeds in their stalls*
> *Stamp and neigh, as the hostler calls;*
> *The day returns, but nevermore*
> *Returns the traveller to the shore,*
> > *And the tide rises, the tide falls.*

The grandfather and grandson would stand quietly at the fingertip of the peninsula. Henry would listen to the rhythm of the sea and its musical pattern of ebb and flow. The crashing of the waves on the rocks sounded like the cymbals of an orchestra. These childhood memories of sound and measured beats might have influenced the meters of his poetry. Learning to play the flute and piano also enhanced his sense of rhythm.

While he heard the music of the sea, he would look at the horizon and dream about the secrets from lands far away.

Then, the man and boy would return to the house on Congress Street for hot drinks in front of the fire. Once Peleg's voice was heard in the house, his grandchildren— Stephen, Elizabeth, Anne, Alexander, Mary, Ellen, and Sam (Henry's siblings)—would run down the stairs and sit at his feet, begging him to tell and retell his adventures in the Revolutionary War.

The grandchildren always asked him about his capture and escape from the British. He, in turn, teased them until they could wait no longer for the story.

Peleg set the scene. After the Siege of Boston was over, General George Washington and his army went south to New York and Pennsylvania. In Maine, the British made a crushing defeat of the Americans, who had to retreat from the Penobscot Valley.

By 1781, General Peleg Wadsworth, the new commander of the American forces in Maine, was tired of war and wanted to resign and return to his family. He had rented a house in Thomaston, Maine, for his wife and two of his children—the others were still in Duxbury, Massachusetts, with grandparents. Battle-fatigued, Peleg went home to discuss his resignation with his wife.

On a February night soon after he arrived home, there was a snowfall. It was dark and quiet. When everyone was asleep, a British troop of twenty-five crashed into the house. Reverend Timothy Dwight recorded these words from Henry's grandmother, Elizabeth Wadsworth, as she described that night, "… the windows dashed, the Doors broken, the House torn to pieces and Blood and Slaughter all around."

Peleg leapt out of bed in his nightshirt and wielded a couple of pistols to ward off his attackers. A bullet struck his left arm and disabled his efforts. He was captured and marched through the snow to a prison in Fort George where the British were encamped. Although locked in a room, Peleg was treated with respect and invited to meals with the officers because of his rank as general. They even allowed his wife to visit him.

At one of these meals, Peleg overheard a discussion about the British leaving for Halifax, Nova Scotia, and sailing to London. Peleg's heart sank. He was afraid they would take him with them and he'd never see his family again. He feared that they even might hang him!

Wadsworth began a plan of escape. He and a fellow prisoner found a small tool and started digging a hole in the ceiling. As the hole became bigger and bigger, they chewed buttered bread—similar in color to the ceiling— and stuffed it into the hole. When the weather became warmer, they were afraid the butter might drip and give away their secret plan.

One night, there was a fierce thunderstorm. Peleg and his prison friend decided to make the break. They tore out the false bread ceiling and scrambled into the rafters. Quietly, they inched their way down the length of the building. Their biggest fear was from the chickens, roosting in the rafters. If the chickens became frightened, they would squawk and send an alarm to their captors. However, the chickens never made a sound. The two men dropped down from the ceiling, escaped through a door, climbed an embankment, clawed their way over a sharp fence, and ran across mud flats into the rainy night. Peleg reached home and never encountered the British again.

After Peleg returned to civilian life, he went to Philadelphia and to Washington, D.C., as a representative in Congress to help form the American government. Once that was done, he came back to Portland and bought 7,800 acres of land between the Saco and Great Ossipee Rivers to raise crops, livestock, and lumber. He built another house—Wadsworth Hall—in a town called Hiram. His original house was built in 1785 and 1786 on Congress Street. It was the first brick house in the town. Peleg ordered the bricks from Philadelphia and had them shipped up the coast to Portland. It took two months for their arrival.

To support his large family, he became a businessman. He brought his hogs and lumber to the Portland harbor and shipped them up and down the coast or to the West Indies.

When the Longfellow grandchildren visited their grandfather Peleg at his big house in Hiram, they continued to ask him to repeat his adventure stories over and over.

* * *

Zilpah Wadsworth, Henry's mother, was lively and sweet. From the age of eight, she was running around the solid brick house on Congress Street. Without today's television, the ten Wadsworth children created their own entertainment. They would gather around the fireplace or sit at the table, studying, drawing, reading their poetry out loud to one another, or singing while their mother, Elizabeth Bartlett Wadsworth, played the spinet piano, but not until their homework was finished.

Because Peleg was such a patriot, he served as a Federalist Representative from Maine from 1792 to 1806 and was gone many months over the winter. He wrote long letters to his wife and children. To the boys, he wrote about business transactions and how to behave in a moral and principled way. Even though they were preteens, he wrote to them like men.

When the teenage sisters, Elizabeth (nicknamed Eliza) and Zilpah, became interested in boys, there was one special boy from Gorham that they both liked. He was Stephen Longfellow IV. His father and grandfather were both graduates of Harvard College. Stephen, too, was a recent graduate of the law school at Harvard and was looking to join or open a law office in Portland.

It was an unusual love story. During his frequent visits to the Wadsworth household, Stephen seemed attracted to the two sisters, Eliza and Zilpah. Zilpah was tall with dark hair and flashing blue eyes. Eliza was fragile and quiet. Eliza seemed to win Stephen's heart, but she became tragically ill with tuberculosis. Zilpah nursed her sister day and night. Stephen came as often as he could and spent long evenings holding Eliza's hand. When she died, Zilpah and Stephen were struck by unspeakable grief.

Their grief drew them closer and they fell in love. They tried to forget their common loss by doing romantic things like going dancing or taking winter sleigh rides or reading and writing poetry. Finally, they married in 1804. And soon, the Longfellows began their own family of eight children in the seaport of Portland, Maine.

When and where would Henry Wadsworth Longfellow come in the line-up of this merger between a Wadsworth daughter and a Longfellow son?

CHAPTER TWO
"Often I think of the beautiful town"
A High Energy Household

2. Wadsworth Longfellow House 1887.
The author's beloved childhood home.
The brick Federal style house was built by Longfellow's grandfather,
General Peleg Wadsworth, after the Revolutionary War.

The newlyweds began their new life together. Of course, they were young and without a great deal of money. Therefore, they rented a house in Portland to establish themselves as a little family.

Although the year 1804 was one of joy for Zilpah and Stephen, it was spoiled by the tragic death of Zilpah's favorite brother, Henry (Harry) Wadsworth. Harry had volunteered to join an American naval expedition to help the French and British defend themselves against pirates, who were raiding ships in the Mediterranean Sea. Harry and his crew were trapped near the port of Tripoli by pirates. The details were sketchy, but Harry's ship was blown up and all lives were lost because they did not want to be enslaved and tortured by the pirates.

The loss of Harry Wadsworth was almost more than his sister could bear. That was all changed in 1805 when her first son was born. The newborn was given the name of Stephen Longfellow to become the fifth Longfellow with that name to carry forward the family tradition.

Stephen's sister, Anne Longfellow Stephenson, was alone in her Portland house while her husband was away at sea. Captain Stephenson invited the young Longfellows to stay in his house to keep his wife company until his return. It was a large house at the east end of Fore Street that looked directly at wharves from its front windows and yard.

Stephen and Zilpah accepted the invitation. On February 27, 1807, their second son was born in that house. In honor of her favorite brother, this baby was named Henry

Wadsworth Longfellow. From the moment he was born, young Henry was like a Mexican jumping bean. He was rarely still and kept his mother running to keep up with him once he could walk. Little Stephen was quieter and moody. Henry, although a handful, had a sunny, happy nature.

By the time Henry was more than one year old, Peleg Wadsworth gave his magnificent brick house on Congress Street to his daughter Zilpah and her growing family. Lucia, Zilpah's younger sister, came to live with them and helped take care of the children and house. They were all thrilled to be back in the Wadsworth house with all its memories.

Stephen Longfellow, like his father-in-law Peleg, found himself away from home a good deal. His training as a lawyer took him to the General Court in Boston and to courtrooms all over Maine.

Communications were by letters in stylish penmanship. Fortunately, letters have been a great source of historical reference for biographers and historians. Today, e-mails are written and deleted, leaving a difficult trail for researchers.

Whenever her husband was away, Zilpah would sit down and write him letters about the family. In one such letter in 1809, she wrote about their delightful, devilish son, Henry, in this way: "A charming little fellow he is. Nothing will do for him but jumping and dancing. He fatigues everyone in the house with tending him."

As a toddler, Henry followed his mother around the house and into their back garden where he played in the dirt while she was planting flowers, having a great time getting himself plastered with mud. There were pear, apple, and plum trees. The garden was Zilpah's favorite place. When Henry's father came home, Henry loved to tag along behind him when he walked through the fields. Everything was an adventure for the bright, curious little boy.

The only way to channel Henry's energy was to put him in school at the age of three. It was a private school run by a woman named Ma'am Fellows. His brother Stephen went to the same school. They would walk there together or sometimes little Henry would be ridden to school by horseback by a black employee of his father.

Life at school for this active child was very hard. He couldn't sit still on the hard wooden benches and was constantly being punished. This meant writing his name on a slate with chalk or performing extra math problems. In those days, calculators weren't in existence. Either counting on one's fingers or using the ancient Chinese abacus was a method of figuring out numbers. However, Henry learned to do math, to read, spell, and write at an age when most American children today just play and make drawings or handicrafts.

By the age of five, Henry was expected to enter public school. Once he began to attend, the boys bullied him. Possibly he was brighter than his peers, making him unpopular.

Henry, finding that the boys at public school were very rough, told his parents of his unhappiness. They removed him and searched for another private school. A young man, Nathaniel Carter, who had graduated from Dartmouth College, opened a small private school. The Longfellows enrolled young Henry and Stephen. Henry turned out to be a happy and eager student.

Mr. Carter sent home a report about Henry that said, "Master Henry is one of the best boys we have in school. He spells and reads very well. He also can add and multiply numbers. His conduct last quarter was very correct and amiable."

Aunt Lucia made some observations about her nephew, which she recorded when he was five years old. Her remarks reflected the influence of the Longfellow household on Henry, regarding their discussions about the War of 1812.

Lucia wrote, "Henry is ready to march, he had his tin gun prepared and his head powdered a week ago." Obviously, Peleg Wadsworth was his role model for such an outfit. Because her father discussed these events with everyone in his family, Zilpah was keenly aware of national and international events. Also her brother's travels abroad, made her curious about life abroad as well as the law cases her husband handled. At the dinner table or in the parlor, the Wadsworths and the Longfellows engaged in lively discussions, which their children overheard. Often they would contribute their own ideas.

Soon Mr. Carter's abilities as an educator were recognized and he was hired by Portland Academy to run their private school. Henry and Stephen were devoted students and switched to Portland Academy, which was a little bigger in size and co-educational. The girls sat on one side of the room and the boys on the other. Henry was shy, but obviously curious about the girls.

But Henry's studies kept him well occupied. Algebra, Greek, and Latin were challenging subjects. According to his brother Samuel, Henry's reading tastes were guided by his mother, who browsed through her husband's library to delight and inspire her son's thirst for reading. She selected the works of Shakespeare, Dryden, Milton, Pope, and other classics. These were authors, playwrights, poets, and philosophers that today might be tackled in high school or college. Henry thought nothing of immersing himself in these books before he was age twelve.

Young Henry Longfellow had a natural love of poetry and committed many of the ballads and poems to memory. Sir Walter Scott's *Marmion* and *Lady of the Lake* caught his attention as did Thomas Moore's *Lalla Rookh* and *The Sketch Book* (his very favorite book) by Washington Irving, whose *Rip Van Winkle* and *The Legend of Sleepy Hollow* were particular favorites. He loved *Don Quixote* and *The Arabian Nights*, too. After dinner and after homework, he would recite them to his siblings and parents, or he would play his flute or the piano.

A schoolmate at Portland Academy wrote these recollections of a young Henry Wadsworth Longfellow.

"I recollect perfectly the impression made upon myself and others. He was a very handsome boy. Retiring, without being reserved, there was a frankness about him that won you at once. He looked you square in the face. His eyes were full of expression, and it seemed as though you could look down into them as into a clear spring ... He had no relish for rude sports; but loved to bathe in a little creek on the border of Deering's Oaks; and would tramp through the woods at times with a gun, but mostly through the influence of others; he loved much better to lie under a tree and read ... If he was thoughtful, he certainly was not a melancholy boy."

The Longfellow household was a high energy one. Zilpah Longfellow patterned the upbringing of her children after that of her own childhood. The family's activities took place in the same parlor where she had grown up.

Of course, there were rainy days in Portland. In the Congress Street kitchen, Henry wrote a poem called *The Rainy Day.*

> *Be still, sad heart; and cease repining*
> *Behind the clouds is the sun still shining.*
> *The fate is the common fate of all,*
> *Into each life some rain must fall.*

Henry lived on the third floor with two of his brothers. Aunt Lucia lived on the third story as well. It was cold in winter up there. The north winds were so fierce that the boys shivered and their teeth chattered on bitterly cold mornings when they quickly jumped into their clothes. The views from their room were incredible. On a clear day, they could see Mt. Washington seventy miles away. From the front windows were views of Casco Bay and the ships, steamboats, and smaller boats sailing in and out during the summer months. These were things to fill a young boy's mind with dreams across the seas.

Amid all this happiness was Henry's first experience at published writing and a stinging criticism. At the age of thirteen, he decided to write a poem about the confrontation between some Indians and Captain Lovell at Lovell's Pond in Fryeburg, Maine. Henry had heard his grandfather tell the story over and over. So, he sat down to write the story in poetic form. He read it to his sister Anne, who thought it was wonderful. He folded it and dropped it off at *The Portland Gazette* without telling his parents. He just signed his first name at the bottom of the poem.

Breathlessly, he waited for it to be published two weeks later. Finally it appeared. He was extremely proud, but too shy to point out the poem to his father.

On the very day it was published, his father took him to visit Judge Mellen, the father of a school friend. Somehow the conversation turned to poetry and the Judge referred Stephen Longfellow to a poem about Lovell's Pond in the local newspaper. Mellen said, "Stiff. Very stiff. Moreover, it was borrowed, every word of it."

Crushed, Henry felt humiliated and couldn't wait to leave. For one thing, he knew that he had not copied his ideas from anyone else. Once back home, his father read the poem. He said it was not very good, but his mother thought otherwise and praised her son.

At other times in his life, Henry had to face criticism about his work from reviewers and other writers, but he learned to listen and not take offense.

At the age of fourteen in 1821, when most boys were entering high school as a freshman, guess what Henry Longfellow was doing?

CHAPTER THREE

"O ye familiar scenes,—ye groves of pines"

Zipping Through Bowdoin College

3. Henry and Stephen stayed at 63 Federal Street in the village of Brunswick, Maine, not too far from the campus. This house would become Harriet Beecher Stowe's residence from 1850–1852, when she wrote the famed *Uncle Tom's Cabin*.

At fourteen, Henry finished his studies and graduated from Portland Academy. His sixteen-year-old brother Stephen also graduated.

They were college bound. Both Henry and Stephen had their hearts set on attending Harvard College. Their relatives on both sides had gone to Harvard. It was *tradition!*

But their father Stephen Longfellow had something else in mind. Because he was a trustee of Bowdoin College, and his own father was a founder of this college (the first college in Maine in 1794) in Brunswick, he decided his sons would go there.

Without any discussion, his sons were informed of this decision. In those days, fathers had the final word in such matters.

However, Zilpah Longfellow was a concerned mother. She wanted to persuade her husband to consider keeping Henry and Stephen at home for their first year in college. She felt that Henry, at the age of fourteen, was too young to leave home. Her husband agreed. Because Stephen was a trustee at Bowdoin, the administration made some adjustments for the Longfellow boys. And so, Henry and Stephen spent their freshman year of college at Portland Academy under the Bowdoin curriculum. Henry was relieved. He really didn't want to leave home, his parents, and all his siblings behind just yet.

Home was the center of everything for Henry. The Longfellow house harbored many happy memories for him. The place was like an old friend and the square brick house was as symmetrical as his poems. There were three stories, enclosing eight rooms. The windows were his eyes to the soul of nature whether to the mountains or bay or the Atlantic gateway to Europe—a continent of the unknown.

Another year in Portland would give Henry time to play in Deering's Woods, where the oaks spread their leafy branches like umbrellas. Henry and his friends laughed and played ball or games there. They carved their initials in the beech trees. All these things of his youth were filed in his memory bank. At the age of forty-eight, Henry Longfellow would write a poem, savoring the days of his carefree youth and the sea fight in the harbor. It was called *My Lost Youth*. Here are some excerpts:

> *Often I think of the beautiful town*
> *That is seated by the sea;*
> *Often in thought go up and down*
> *The pleasant streets of that dear old town.*
> *And my youth comes back to me.*

* * *

> *I remember the black wharves and the slips,*
> *And the sea-tides tossing free;*

* * *

I remember the bulwarks by the shore,
And the fort upon the hill;

* * *

I remember the sea-fight far away,
How it thundered o'er the tide!

* * *

I can see the breezy dome of groves,
The shadow of Deering's Woods

The year passed quickly for the two college boys. In the fall of 1822, it was time to pack their things and head thirty miles north to Brunswick, Maine, and to the small campus of Bowdoin College. Stephen Longfellow accompanied his two sons to get them settled.

Like any mother in any century, Zilpah Longfellow wept while saying her goodbyes to Henry and Stephen. It was hard to see her sons grow up and leave the tight circle of the family. She reminded them to write their parents and siblings with news of their activities and college courses. Henry said that he would. Stephen avoided the question.

They climbed into the stagecoach and began the five hour journey to their college environment. It was exciting, but a little scary; especially for fifteen-year-old Henry. Stephen, on the other hand, was looking forward to his freedom.

Once they arrived, Stephen Longfellow discovered that all the dormitories were full, leaving no space for his two sons. Quickly, the concerned father found a room at a minister's home where both boys could share a rather starkly furnished room. It had only a double bed for them to share, a little washstand, two uncomfortable chairs, and a smoky fireplace. The Reverend's house was at 63 Federal Street in the village of Brunswick, not too far from the campus. The boys took all their meals at the minister's residence.

This house would become Harriet Beecher Stowe's residence from 1850–1852, when she wrote the famed *Uncle Tom's Cabin*. Incidentally, Henry wrote anti-slavery poems almost a decade before Stowe's book. Upon meeting the famous author, Stowe, Abraham Lincoln remarked, "So you are the lady who started the war."

The Bowdoin campus is set on a small hill above the town of Brunswick. There were only a few buildings on the quadrangle in 1822 when Henry arrived. Styled in simple Federal architecture of red brick, Massachusetts Hall housed the Trustees and Overseers for their somber meetings in a room large enough to hold a long dark table, surrounded by hard-backed chairs. The chapel spire dominated the campus where the students were required to meet every morning.

North College (now Maine Hall) was the dormitory where the brothers lived in their junior and senior years. It was a third floor room, looking out on pine woods.

The tall, cone-shaped fir trees spread their branches like a ladder, climbing to the top of the pine pyramid. The sea breezes from several miles away softly fluttered their evergreen fingers. Pine needles fell to the grassy floor beneath them, filling the campus with their woodsy scent.

From the north end of Maine Street at the edge of campus, the road still slides gently down to the village. Alongside the slope is its green mall.

Their schedule started early. They had to be at Chapel at 6:00 a.m., followed by their first class. Starving, they rushed back for breakfast and went to class again at 11:00 a.m. Dinner was served at the Reverend's table at midday before they returned at 2:00 p.m. for more classes. Evening prayers concluded the day.

In the evenings, students were not allowed to leave their rooms. Stephen Longfellow violated that rule frequently by stealing out of the clergyman's house and going to the local tavern in town. This was a problem for Henry. He couldn't tell the school or his parents about his brother, so he turned a blind eye to his brother's antics. Instead, Henry made friends of his own.

There were two literary societies on campus and Henry joined the one called "Peucinians," named for the pine woods in town. Nathaniel Hawthorne belonged to the "Athenaeum," which explains why they were not friends until after college. Henry and his society friends would stroll into the pine woods, discussing the literary works they were reading inside and outside of the classroom.

Henry was particularly taken by an 18th century English poet by the name of Thomas Gray. He wrote long letters to his mother, expressing his enchantment, although his professor was not that keen on the poet. Zilpah would read some of the same works and had a lively correspondence with her son about them. Henry also stumbled upon a history book, describing the bad treatment of Native Americans in Pennsylvania. He later revealed his sensitivity to other cultures in his poem, *The Song of Hiawatha*. Here is a brief extract:

> *I am weary of your quarrels,*
> *Weary of your wars and bloodshed,*
> *Weary of your prayers for vengeance,*
> *Of your wranglings and dissension;*
> *All your strength is in your union,*
> *All your danger is in discord;*
> *Therefore, be at peace henceforward,*
> *And as brothers live together.*

This is what a Bowdoin classmate, Bradbury, had to say about Henry Longfellow, "I met him for the first time in the autumn of 1822, when I entered as a Sophomore, the class of which he was a member. As we both had our rooms out of college and in the same vicinity, we were often together in passing to and from the recitation room, and became well acquainted. He was genial, sociable, and agreeable, and always a gentleman in his deportment. He had a happy temperament, free from envy and every corroding passion and vice. His figure was slight and erect. His nose was prominent, his eyes clear and blue and his well-formed head covered with a profusion of brown hair waving loosely."

Professor Packard described Henry this way, "An attractive youth, of well-bred manners and bearing...of unblemished character as a pupil, and a true gentleman in all his relations with the college and its teachers."

During his junior and senior years at Bowdoin, Henry was beginning to feel his independence. One February vacation he traveled to Boston to attend a gala ball, given by a Miss Emily Marshall. There he danced with the Russian consul's daughter. Because of his amiable personality and many talents, he was a desirable guest. While in Boston, he visited the Navy Yard, the astounding Athenaeum Library, and the studio of local artist Gilbert Stuart. He saw many sites in Cambridge and his world was enlarging.

Although young men of the 1800s turned to their fathers for guidance in career choices, Henry Longfellow was afraid that his father's choice for him would be the wrong one. His brother Stephen was going into law like his father.

As graduation approached for the forty-five members in the class of 1825, Henry wrote to his father, "I am curious to know what you intend to make of me—whether I am to study a profession or not: and if so, what profession. I hope your ideas upon this subject will agree with mine, for I have a particular and strong prejudice, for one course of life, to which you, I fear, will not agree. It will not be worth while for me to mention what this is, until I become more acquainted with your own wishes."

Obviously, Henry was trying to be respectful, but paving the way for presenting his own desires. His father's reply indicated that he should consider a career in law or medicine or the ministry.

Henry made a forceful answer to his father, "... in thinking to make a lawyer of me, I fear you thought more partially than justly. I do not for my own part imagine that such a coat would suit me. I hardly think Nature designed me for the bar, or the pulpit, or the dissecting room ... I want to spend one year at Cambridge for the purpose of reading history, and of becoming familiar with the best authors in polite literature: while at the same time I can be acquiring knowledge of the Italian language, without an acquaintance with which I shall be shut out from one of the most beautiful departments of letters. The French I mean to understand pretty thoroughly before I leave college. After leaving Cambridge, I would attach myself to some literary periodical publication, by which I could maintain myself and still enjoy the advantages in reading."

Here was the real purpose of his letter to his father, ".... the fact is, and I will not disguise it in the least, for I think I ought not, the fact is, I most eagerly aspire after future eminence in literature: my whole soul burns most ardently for it, and every earthly thought centers in it."

Stephen Longfellow was not pleased with his son's desire to pursue a career in literature. He didn't think it was possible to earn a living in such a field. They compromised and agreed that Henry would spend a year of graduate work at Harvard.

Throughout his college years, Henry submitted poetry to a number of poetry magazines. *The United States Literary Gazette* received 24 of his poems and published most of them. Sometimes he was paid and sometimes he wasn't.

Meanwhile, Henry was getting ready to graduate fourth in his class. He was astonished and rather modest about learning that news, "How I came to get so high is rather a mystery to me, inasmuch as I have never been a remarkably hard student, touching college studies, except during my sophomore year, when I used to think I was studying pretty hard."

The day after the September graduation, Henry read from a speech he had written about Native Writers. "To an American, there is something endearing in the very sound—Our Native Writers. Like the music of our native tongue, when heard in a foreign land, they have the power to kindle up within him, the tender memory of his home and fireside; and more than this, they foretell that whatever is noble and attractive in our national character will one day be associated with the sweet magic of Poetry ... already a spirit and love of literature are springing up in the shadow of our free political institutions."

Perhaps these lyrical phrases were a forecast of Henry's future.

Although sorry to leave their friends, the two brothers were glad to leave the hard winters in Brunswick. Henry and Stephen loaded their belongings into a stagecoach and returned to Portland with their mother and two siblings that attended the graduation ceremonies. Their father stayed behind for a Trustees' meeting.

After Stephen returned home, he gathered the whole family together in the parlor and made a surprising announcement. Their son Henry had been appointed the new chair of modern languages at Bowdoin.

No one was more surprised than young Henry. He wanted to know how the college decided on this position for such a new graduate. His father explained that Mrs. James Bowdoin—widow of Bowdoin's founder—had given a thousand dollars for this very purpose. Furthermore, Benjamin Orr—one of Henry's professors—had been impressed by Henry's translation from Latin into English of one of Horace's odes (a Roman poet in 65 B.C.). Orr also noted and praised Henry's expertise in the French language.

However, Bowdoin's offer of the professorship had one condition. They wanted Henry to spend a year in Europe, perfecting his knowledge of French, Spanish, German, and Italian.

Young Henry was ecstatic about going to Europe. He had always dreamed of these distant places across the

Atlantic Ocean. But his enthusiasm was dampened by his father's proposal. Because Stephen would pay $600 for the year abroad, he insisted that Henry work in his law office between the fall of 1825 and the spring of 1826.

The whole family was thrilled. They cheered and sang. Zilpah was a little sad, but happy for her son. Henry could hardly believe this new experience was going to happen to him.

How soon would Henry leave on his adventure?

CHAPTER FOUR

"Filled is Life's goblet to the brim;"

Trekking Across Europe

4. Longfellow found Rome captivating.

Time passed very slowly for Henry. Working at his father's law office was not only boring, but unappetizing to the sensitive poet. Whenever possible, Henry would sneak away to a quiet room to write a poem for the *Literary Gazette* or to study French.

As his departure date drew closer, Stephen Longfellow wrote letters of introduction to his friends in Boston and Northampton, Massachusetts, as contacts for his son, hoping they would offer good advice and provide contacts abroad for him.

Henry's spring departure from Portland in 1826 was exciting for the nineteen-year-old. But the prospect of their son leaving home and country for Europe and for an absence of at least a year, according to Bowdoin's Board of Overseers, was a concern for his parents.

Boston and Cambridge were familiar to Henry. He immediately visited Professor George Ticknor, chair of Harvard's modern language department. Ticknor was delighted about the young man's plans for Europe. He gave him letters of introduction, including one to author Washington Irving in Spain. Ticknor also suggested Henry study German at the University of Gottingen in Germany.

The stagecoach route to New York City went from Boston to Northampton and on to Albany, New York, where Henry caught a boat down the Hudson River to New York City. At Northampton, he contacted several of his father's friends, who agreed with Ticknor's advice.

There, he visited his good friend George Pierce, who was studying law.

Once in New York City, Henry discovered that his ship *Cadmus* wouldn't be leaving until mid-May. He headed to Philadelphia to do a little sightseeing and was disturbed by the sights at a hospital for the poor. It made such an impression on him that he included it in his long poem *Evangeline*.

> *And, with light in her looks, she entered the chambers of sickness.*
> *Noiselessly moved about the assiduous, careful attendants,*
> *Moistening the feverish lip, and the aching brow, and in silence*
> *Closing the sightless eyes of the dead, and concealing their faces,*
> *Where on their pallets they lay, like drifts of snow by the roadside.*

Back at the New York port, Henry found two letters awaiting him—one from his mother and one from his father.

As expected, his mother was much more sentimental in her words to her son. "I will not say how much we miss your elastic step, your cheerful voice, your melodious flute. I will say, farewell, my dear son, may God be with you and prosper you. May you be successful in your pursuit of knowledge; may you hold fast to your integrity, and retain that purity of heart which is so endearing to your friends. I feel as if you were going into a thousand perils."

Stephen Longfellow's letter contained wise advice. "It is impossible, with all my solicitude, to give you all the instructions which your youth and inexperience require; but permit me to conjure you to remember the objects of your journey and keep them constantly in view ... Be careful not to take any part in opposition to the religion or politics of the countries in which you reside. They are local concerns, in which a stranger has no right to interfere. I want to say a thousand things, but the time for the mail to close has arrived. In all your ways remember the God by whose power you were created, by whose goodness you are sustained and protected."

On the deck of the ship, Henry felt a lump in his throat and tears filling his eyes as the ship turned to the open seas toward the coast of France where he would arrive in a month's time. A fleeting feeling of homesickness encircled his heart.

The people on board were mostly French. They chattered so rapidly that Henry couldn't keep up and realized his studies at school were useless when it came to conversational French. The purpose of his trip became even stronger.

Once he arrived at Le Havre de Grace at the mouth of the Seine River, Henry expected to jump off and catch a steamer to Rouen where he wished to see the place of the trial and execution of Joan of Arc as well as the tomb of Britain's Richard the Lion Hearted. Instead, he was caught in the officialdom of red tape. The customs officials wanted to examine his papers more carefully, which delayed Henry for a full day.

Nevertheless, he observed the peculiarities of Le Havre through American and a New Englander's eyes. The police grew thick black whiskers and the women wore white muslin hats that soared two feet into the air, and they shuffled around town in wooden shoes. Laundry hung from the upper windows of homes, drying in the sea winds. All of these strange sights amused Henry.

Finally, he was free to continue his journey. It was too late to catch a steamer and he resorted to the public stagecoach that bumped its way to Rouen. The Gothic architecture of the Rouen Cathedral amazed him. The simplicity of the First Parish Unitarian Church in Portland, where his family attended, was so different from the ornate architecture, stained glass windows, and the complex rituals of the services at the Rouen Cathedral. From Rouen, he boarded another stagecoach to Paris.

Upon arriving, Henry contacted a distant cousin, Ebenezer Storer, who had reserved a room for him at Madame Potel's, located at 49 Rue Monsieur-le-Prince. It was not far from the Luxembourg Gardens and cost him $36 a month for both room and board. There were seven American boarders and none of them were allowed to speak English at mealtimes. Otherwise, they were fined.

Naturally, Henry was dazzled by Paris. He described it to his brother as a carnival atmosphere, going on night and day. With his eyes opened wide and a jaw that nearly dropped at the magnificent sites, Henry ran from one end of Paris to the other. He popped into ancient bookstores to browse, watched the operations of printing shops, and strolled down the broad boulevards. He was in heaven!

With an eye for fine and colorful clothes, he had a long burgundy dress coat made along with linen pantaloons. He even bought a glossy black hat. Only to his brother did he write about these exotic discoveries and purchases, but obviously, Stephen shared the letter with his parents.

Henry's father was alarmed and wrote, "It seems that you have changed your costume to that of a Parisian ... You will find it expensive to you, as your French dress would be useless to you in Spain, or any other country;"

Quickly Henry responded to his father by saying it was all a joke, "... what clothes I have had made was all after the English model."

Both his parents wrote to admonish their son; especially his father, "Your expenses are much more than I had been led to expect; and though I wish you to appear respectably you will recollect the necessity of observing as much economy as you can with propriety. And as your great object is to acquire knowledge of the modern languages, the importance of great diligence will strongly impress your mind and influence your conduct."

These letters took three months to travel across the seas and by stagecoach to reach their destinations. But they made an impression.

Before the letters of parental disapproval arrived, Henry indulged himself in attending French theatre; particularly the Comedie Francaise, where he developed a schoolboy crush on the star, Mademoiselle Mars. He also became smitten with opera, a passion that never left him. Henrietta Sontag, a famous soprano, was a favorite and Henry would meet her years later when she was performing in Boston.

When the family letters arrived, Henry decided to get down to business and start perfecting his French. Some of the French passengers on the trip across the Atlantic had suggested a place for him to stay in a village called Auteuil, three miles outside of Paris. To escape the Parisian summer, he went to Auteuil and found a room at a convalescent home. Determined to make the best of it, Henry began conversing in French with many of the patients. Auteuil was located along the Seine River and was near a village where Benjamin Franklin had once stayed.

After the summer was over, Henry returned to Paris and stayed with a French family at 5 Rue Racine, near his former lodgings. Since the Parisian family spoke no English, Henry was forced to immerse himself in French. While waiting for lectures to start in Paris, he hiked through the Loire Valley, starting from Orleans, enjoying the rich vineyards, lush green hills, and large chateaux before returning to the French family quarters.

Having spent eight months in Paris, Henry received a letter from his father, urging him to go to Spain and start learning the language. The elder Longfellow could foresee that his son could very well enter the diplomatic branch of government. He told his son that relations between the United States and South America were growing and a command of the Spanish language could be useful.

When Washington Irving's nephew, Pierre Irving, returned from Spain to Paris, Henry met and talked with him about the safety of traveling around Spain. Pierre urged him to go, which he decided to do. Despite civil war and highway robberies there, Henry felt inspired to continue his plans.

In February of 1827, Henry packed his belongings, stuffing his beloved flute in his backpack. He took a series of stagecoaches that put him in Spain on his birthday, February 27, marking his twentieth year. For a few moments he was seized with homesickness for his home and family. He put those thoughts aside and focused on observing the Spanish people and culture.

The border between Spain and France was filled with such poverty that Henry was caught up in sympathetic emotions. Everywhere he looked, there were black crosses along the road where people had been murdered.

Madrid was lively and colorful. The food was spicy and delicious. It was 1,800 feet above sea level and delighted Henry. Fortunately, his father sent him more funds to keep him well supplied during his time in Spain.

Before taking a room with a Spanish family in Madrid, Henry and a friend of Pierre Irving's, Lieutenant Alexander Slidel, journeyed to the old town of Segovia, northwest of Madrid in a mountainous and dangerous area.

From there they went to Escorial where they found a famous monastery, filled with an art collection and library, established by Philip II in the 16th century.

Back in Madrid, Henry finally met his idol, Washington Irving, whom he found to be witty and friendly. At the time of Henry's visit, the author was working on a book about the life of Columbus. His brother Peter Irving was there, too. Henry also admired and copied Irving's work ethic of beginning his work day at 6:00 a.m.

During the summer, Henry traveled around central Spain, indulging himself in watching and participating in local folk dances. He loved the color and music of Spain; especially the exotic flamenco dances. The flashing dark eyes and shiny black hair of Spanish women attracted him. He was fascinated by their long black braids that fell to the middle of their backs. The Basque women along the border between Spain and France were intriguing, exciting, and mesmeric!

After nine months in Spain, Henry began his final journeys through southern Spain. Somehow, he was unimpressed by Seville and its many monuments and churches. However, he was spellbound by the port city of Cadiz, the sunny beaches of Malaga, and the many conquests of Granada. The round, 13th century Alhambra Palace in Granada with its Moorish architecture had a great impact on him. All in all, he found Spain very romantic. Because he didn't want to spoil his memories, Henry never returned to Spain in future trips.

Soon he traveled to Great Britain's Rock of Gibraltar, which is the gateway to the Mediterranean Sea. From there, he sailed to Genoa, Italy, which he found enchanting. Remembering his father's concerns, he went directly to Florence for a month. The Renaissance art history was enriching. He visited the Pitti Palace and many beautiful art galleries. But most of all there were gala balls and theatrical plays to see. As in Spain, Henry found himself attracted to the peasant women.

Seeking warmer weather, Henry traveled to Rome in January of 1828. By now, he had been away from home for more than a year and a half. But his pursuit of learning modern languages had not been completed. He still had to master Italian and German. On the other hand, what could his parents do? He was away from their control and having a jolly good time while learning the languages!

Henry found Rome captivating. The Roman Forum and Coliseum were monuments of incredible historic value. The Italian accent or dialect in Rome seemed softer and more melodic to his ear.

For lodgings, Henry stayed with the Persiani family, whose three daughters helped him learn Italian. Because of his knowledge of the Spanish language, he found Italian fairly easy to learn. George Greene of Rhode Island had found this lodging for him. George was the grandson of Nathaniel Greene, George Washington's most trusted general in the Revolutionary War.

The two young men traveled to Naples to see the ruins of Pompeii and the volcano Mt. Vesuvius, which they viewed from their balcony. They continued through southern Italy, spying out many historic and beautiful sites such as Sorrento and the Isle of Capri.

By now, Stephen Longfellow was becoming impatient with his son's lengthy stay and wanted to know why he wasn't in Germany.

Part of the reason Henry didn't leave Italy was his budding love for Julia, one of the three sisters in the Persiani family. But when his father wrote that Bowdoin had changed its mind about his professorship, cut the payment in half and made it Instructor, not Professor, Henry was jolted out of his love-stricken state and began his journey to Germany.

Henry paused in Venice for five days. Naturally he was overwhelmed by its architectural beauty and its romantic network of canals. One day he was sketching the Bridge of Sighs when a maid threw out a pail of water from a high window and drenched his head and clothes. Though startled, he laughed it off. Venice was full of surprises! He was particularly interested in the Palace of the Doges with its dark, damp dungeons.

Perhaps the most interesting part of Venice to Henry was a visit to a literary salon held by Madame Benzon, an elderly lady. It began at 11:30 p.m. and lasted until two or three in the morning. Her house had been a favorite visiting place of the English poet Lord Byron.

Mindful of his father's warning to get to Germany and learn the language, Henry left Venice for Verona before heading to Dresden, Germany, where Washington Irving had provided contacts.

Socially, Dresden was engaging and Henry loved conversing in German with locals. Soon he discovered that his social life was interfering with his intense study of the language.

From Dresden, he wrote to Carey and Lea, publishers in Philadelphia, explaining to them that he intended to write Sketches and Tales of New England for them when he returned. Ironically, after three years in Europe, his next writing project would be about New England—a surprising decision. Perhaps his absence from that section of America sharpened his images of it.

To his sisters, he wrote, "By every language you learn, a new world is opened before you. It is like being born again."

The University of Gottingen was his final destination. There were no distractions. He buckled down to study. Ned Preble, a neighbor from Portland and a classmate from Bowdoin, was also there. Henry intensified his study of German, which he found easy to read, but difficult to write.

In their spare time, Longfellow and Preble produced a weekly student newspaper in a variety of languages. It was full of sophomoric satire and stinging jabs at Bowdoin. Henry took out his anger on professors and trustees at Bowdoin by making fun of them in his poems and cartoons. Being so far away from isolated Bowdoin, the two graduates felt safe in attacking them.

Over spring break, Henry took a boat down the Rhine River, enjoying the castles along the bluffs. He crossed to London, England, before returning to Gottingen via Rotterdam in Holland.

But Europe, after three years, was losing its attraction. It was time to go home. Yet, he had savored every moment, each of which would influence his future writings.

Receiving news of his sister Elizabeth's illness quickened his departure. Another letter from his father, telling of her death, was devastating. Henry boarded the ship *Manchester* in Liverpool, England, to return to American shores. He reached New York on August 11, 1829.

How would Henry be received back in Portland after three expensive years away from his home?

CHAPTER FIVE

"… how much she possesses of all we most admire in
a female character!"

A Lively Professor and Getting Married

5. Mary Storer Potter Longfellow, unknown artist, c. 1830

All was forgiven when Henry entered his boyhood home in Portland and was embraced by everyone in his family. The joy of seeing their wandering scholar washed away all worries and parental unhappiness concerning Henry's $2,600 of expenses over three years. Henry Longfellow was now a well-traveled man of the world—at least of Europe.

The grief the family had experienced over the loss of Elizabeth was written on their faces. His parents never truly recovered from the death of their daughter. Zilpah, Lucia, and Anne were responsible for nursing and caring for Elizabeth throughout her struggle against tuberculosis.

Elizabeth's fiancé, William Pitt Fessenden, also had endured his own grief and pain over the loss of his bride-to-be. Nevertheless, he was inspired by her courage right to the end. Eventually he married Ellen Deering and had an illustrious life, including becoming Abraham Lincoln's Secretary of the Treasury.

To distract the family from their grief, Henry kept them entertained by describing all his adventures during his colorful journey around Europe. He held them spellbound and made them laugh, easing their sadness. It was a great sense of regret that his letter to Elizabeth didn't reach her before her passing and that he didn't arrive to see her one last time.

But Henry Longfellow's immediate need was to find employment rather quickly to start supporting himself. It was the end of August and Bowdoin's fall term would soon begin.

Stephen was amazed by his son's confident approach to the Trustees of Bowdoin after their original offer of salary had been reduced to $600 because of the unexpected length of his stay in Europe.

Henry wrote,

> Dear Sir:
> Your letter to my father dated Sept. 26, 1828, and enclosing a copy of the vote of the Trustees and Overseers of Bowdoin College, by which they have elected me Instructor of Modern Languages in that institution, has been duly handed me. I am sorry, that under existing circumstances, I cannot accept the appointment. The Professorship of Modern Languages, with a salary equal to that of other Professors, would certainly not have been refused. But having at great expense, devoted four years to the acquisition of the French, Spanish, Italian and German languages, I cannot accept a subordinate station with a salary so disproportionate to the duties required.
> I have the honor to be, Sir,
>
> Very respectfully
> Your Obedient Servant
> Henry W. Longfellow

Surprised at Henry's skill and courage, Stephen did not object to the tone of Henry's letter and agreed to his sending it.

Taken off-guard by Henry's response, but desperate to hire Longfellow to teach modern languages, the Overseers made a more substantial offer, consisting of $800 plus $100 to become librarian for an hour a day.

Stephen and Henry were delighted with the outcome. Henry accepted the offer and packed his belongings. Once again he would be back at Bowdoin's familiar campus.

Being a well-traveled professor was quite different from being a student. Henry bristled at being so far away from the activity of a city. He even suggested to his father that an extension of the College should be in Portland. Confined to the remote location of Bowdoin was an adjustment for him.

His living arrangements were in the college halls, but he took meals with a family. In a letter to his friend George Greene, Henry confessed to not liking the society there in general, preferring to become friends with only three families on campus. He was especially fond of Professor Parker Cleveland and his family. Perhaps the three daughters were an attraction.

Furthermore, he was caught in the middle of a political storm. Funding for the college came from the Maine legislature. They put their own appointees in charge. As a result, the administration was facing a religious warfare over the control of the college. The Congregationalists were challenging the Unitarians for control. Bowdoin had always been liberal in its thinking whether in religion or politics. But until Bowdoin declared itself a private institution, the churches had no power. Once Bowdoin became private, the Congregationalists raised the most money to support the college and therefore, had the most power.

Henry steered away from this issue and concentrated on his teaching. His students were thrilled to have such a young professor who understood them. In the library, they often sought his advice on literature and authors. He always dropped everything to help them. His popularity increased so much that by the second year, 52 students signed up for his courses.

One of his students commented upon Professor Longfellow, "... I mentioned as a proposed subject some philosophical errors of the Middle Ages. He entered into the idea at once with interest, and afterwards complimented my poor performance altogether beyond the truth. It was his way. He was never insincere, but his ready and hearty sympathy with every honest effort would betray him into language that had its degree of truth in his feelings."

Early in the term, Henry discovered that the textbooks for teaching French and Spanish were unbearably boring and dull. He wanted his students to be interested and enjoy learning these modern languages.

To capture their attention, he translated his own little textbook from a French grammar. Then, he began translating French proverbs, which were a series of seven

French plays. He turned them into textbooks as well. He did the same with Spanish. In fact, he took Washington Irving's *Rip Van Winkle* and *The Young Italian* and translated them into Italian. The local printer in Brunswick, Joseph Griffin, printed 500 copies for him at a cost of $72. Henry paid out of his own money and then recovered his costs when the students bought the textbooks from him.

Although these new small textbooks weren't great works of literature, they created student interest on an understandable level, making it easier to learn the language. Professor Ticknor at Harvard was impressed with them, but more impressed at the industriousness of the new young professor.

Somehow a publisher in Boston, Gray and Bowen, heard about Henry's books in several languages and began to publish them, which was a great thrill to young Longfellow.

In the fall of 1830, Henry gave his inaugural address as a new professor. The topic was "The Origin and Growth of the Languages of Southern Europe and of their Literature." At the beginning of his speech, he expressed gratitude to everyone for his appointment as Professor of Modern Languages. He also revealed his motive for being a teacher.

"I cannot help believing that he who bends in the right direction the pliant disposition of the young, and trains up the ductile mind to a vigorous and healthy growth does something for the welfare of his country and something for the great interests of humanity."

Another portion of the speech hinted at a spiritual viewpoint, "It is this religious feeling,—this changing of the finite for the infinite, this constant grasping after the invisible things of another and a higher world,—which marks the spirit of modern literature."

In writing to his friend, George Greene, Longfellow described the details of his daily teaching.

"I rise at six in the morning, and hear a French recitation of Sophomores immediately. At seven I breakfast, and am then master of my time until eleven, when I hear a Spanish lesson of Juniors. After that I take a lunch; and at twelve I go into the library, where I remain till one. I am then at leisure for the afternoon till five, when I have a French recitation of Juniors. At six, I take coffee; then walk and visit friends till nine; study till twelve, and sleep till six, when I begin the same round again. Such is the daily routine of my life. The intervals of college duty I fill up with my own studies."

One of these intervals was to write articles for *The North American Review*. Longfellow had met the editor, Alexander Everett, in Madrid when Everett was Minister to Spain.

Although everything was progressing splendidly in his professional life, Henry longed for female companionship. His friends Pierre Irving and George Greene had both married. The young bachelor began traveling more frequently to Portland. At one of the services at the First Parish Unitarian Church, he had spotted a lovely young woman by the name of Mary Storer Potter. Her father,

Judge Barrett Potter, was a friend of Henry's father, and they were neighbors.

Though Mary was five years younger than Henry, they both had attended Portland Academy. This young lady was well-educated in Latin and Greek. Henry was struck by her shy charm, by her dark-haired beauty, and by her brilliant blue eyes.

A whirlwind courtship began. Judge Potter was an overprotective father, so Henry had to send secret love notes to Mary through his sister Anne. Eventually they became engaged in September of 1830. Like a man truly in love, Henry sent a letter to Mary's widowed father that expressed his feelings about his daughter.

"... her pure heart and guileless disposition ... I have never seen a woman in whom every look, and word, and action seemed to proceed from so gentle and innocent a spirit. Indeed, how much she possesses of all we most admire in a female character!"

Apparently, Mary was as deeply in love as Henry. She couldn't bear to be parted from him. Zilpah and Stephen heartily approved of the couple's engagement. They were married in September of 1831.

What about Henry's poetry? He hadn't written one verse since before he left for Europe. Would he ever pick up his quill pen again?

CHAPTER SIX

"Into each life some rain must fall"

Return to Europe and Unexpected Grief

6. After their marriage, the Longfellow couple settled into Brunswick, Maine, to begin a new life near Bowdoin College.

After their marriage, the Longfellow couple settled into Brunswick, Maine, to begin a new life near Bowdoin College.

The newlyweds stayed in a boarding house on Federal Street until they found a charming Cape-style cottage to rent. It was set under tall elm trees and surrounded by honeysuckle bushes. It was idyllic.

Decades later, when General Joshua L. Chamberlain (of Civil War fame) became President of Bowdoin College, he took this very cottage and moved it to the corner of Maine and Potter Streets in 1867. However, Chamberlain had the cottage made into the second-story of his new home. Today, it still remains a historic site for Chamberlain and Longfellow.

According to historical documents, Henry Longfellow revisited the upper story of that house during his 50th Bowdoin reunion and reportedly wept upon seeing the familiar rooms where he and Mary began their married life. He recalled writing poetry there, staring into the flames of the sitting room fireplace.

Henry was delighted with married life. Zilpah described Mary as "a very lovely woman, very affectionate and amiable." One of his greatest joys was his study on the ground floor of their little home. The atmosphere of his study transported him to Spain. He wrote about the shadows of a honeysuckle bush that fell upon his study floor. In spring and summer, the sounds of birds and sweet aroma of honeysuckle filled his ears and nostrils, reminding him of the sounds and smells of central and southern Spain.

Since he was still librarian at Bowdoin, Henry ordered books for the college library as well as for his own home library. Books were his "passion and delight." That passion remained throughout his life.

Besides his heavy schedule of teaching, Henry made time to write articles for *The North American Review*. He wrote features on "The Defence of Poetry" and "The Moral and Devotional Poetry of Spain." In total, he produced six articles for them. Some were translations of pieces from French and Italian. At the same time, he was preparing lectures for his students on the Literary History from the Middle Ages.

For *The New England Magazine*, Henry developed a series of "Sketches," which were really descriptive vignettes of his wanderings in France. They were written under the title of "Schoolmaster."

This series eventually became a two volume hardcover book in 1835, published by Harper and Brothers in New York. It is a book about Henry's complete travels in Europe, called *Outre-Mer*, which means Land Beyond the Sea. The full title is *A Pilgrimage Beyond the Sea*. His father didn't like the title at all, but Henry said that Europe was considered the Holy Land—a name given by traveling pilgrims. Henry would not be dissuaded from the title.

The volumes were published first as pamphlets without his name attached. There was a strong criticism from a reviewer, saying the anonymous writer had stolen a story about a friar and claimed it as original. It was not Henry's habit to respond to criticism, but in this case, he did. Like most authors, Longfellow kept a scrapbook of reviews about his books.

Even with all this activity, Henry felt imprisoned by the isolation in Brunswick and by his tight academic schedule. He missed the freedom of Europe and its peoples. However, a trip to Boston with Mary in winter helped break the monotony of his scholarly life; especially when they visited with Professor Ticknor at Harvard.

Finally, after eight years, the dry period of not writing poetry was broken. In 1832 the Phi Beta Kappa Chapter (a high academic honor society) at Bowdoin invited Longfellow to write a poem for Commencement. Suddenly the poetic juices began to flow. He wrote four hundred lines. The reception of the poem at the ceremonies was overwhelmingly positive. So much so, that the Chapter in Cambridge wanted him to repeat his performance in August of 1833 at their Chapter meeting.

In preparation, Henry made some changes. The title was "Past and Present" with an emphasis on Education. At first, Henry had been told that John Quincy Adams would also be a speaker. However, famed orator Edward Everett spoke instead. They both received an abundance of praise.

While these praises were rewarding, Henry found that his restlessness with Bowdoin was increasing. There was internal friction within the administration of the college, which disturbed Henry. Therefore, he began casting around for another position elsewhere. There was an opening as headmaster at the Round Hill School in Northampton, Massachusetts, but Mary was opposed to that move. His true desire was to write poetry and prose as a fulltime profession, but finances did not permit that choice.

In this mood of inner turmoil, Henry was unaware of the impending retirement of his friend Professor Ticknor from Harvard, until a special letter, written in December of 1834, arrived. It was a letter from the President of Harvard College, Josiah Quincy, offering Henry the position of the Professor of Modern Languages at Harvard.

Apparently, Ticknor had written a letter of recommendation to the President about Henry Longfellow. Ticknor encouraged Quincy to strongly consider this talented young scholar as his successor.

However, in the letter to Longfellow, Quincy said that he would need to spend a year or more in Europe at his own expense, perfecting his German and learning the Scandinavian languages. Further, the letter said that Professor Ticknor agreed to stay at his post until Henry returned. Also, the salary offered to Longfellow would amount to $1,500 for the year and of course, would require him to live in Cambridge.

Longfellow was filled with unbounded joy and he accepted the offer wholeheartedly. His growing anxieties at Bowdoin disappeared. Even Mary was excited, but a little apprehensive about being away so long. Henry started to plan their itinerary immediately and informed Bowdoin of his departure in March for Europe and of his new post at Harvard.

In April 1835, a party of four met in New York to board a ship for England with travel plans for Scandinavia, Holland, and Germany. Henry had selected two young ladies, friends of his wife, to accompany them, so that Mary could have some company when he was researching, studying, and exploring. They were Mary Goddard, whose father promised to pay his daughter's expenses upon their return, and Clara Crowninshield, who had her own private fortune.

Clara had a very keen perception of character. In her diary, she recorded these observations about Mary Longfellow, "She is very sweet and amiable, but she is so absorbed in her husband that she only lives in him. She has not much physical energy and if her husband only goes about and sees what is worth seeing, she is satisfied to have it secondhand thro' him. Now I want to have somebody go who will excite instead of check any desire I may have to go about and improve myself."

Once they landed in Portsmouth, England, the four went to London where Longfellow wanted to stay for a month. His main purpose was to circulate with well-known British writers. The result was not what he expected.

His breakfast with English writer Sir John Bowring was disappointing. Bowring totally ignored Longfellow at the table. He was only interested in reading his mail and not in engaging in conversation with the American poet. The only animation Bowring displayed was in showing Longfellow his own bust being created in his library. For Henry, the whole experience was extremely rude and very offensive.

In the company of several other English writers, he was also rejected by their superior attitudes toward him. However, an invitation to the home of Charles Babbage, a renowned mathematician, salvaged the situation. There, Babbage showed the guests his invention of a monstrous machine, supposed to be a calculator (and perhaps an early forerunner of the 20th century computer). Another evening at the home of Lady Dudley Stuart was even more agreeable. There were operatic songs from the Italian composer Rossini. This was sheer pleasure for Longfellow.

Their sightseeing tours to art galleries more than made up for the unpleasant reception Longfellow received from British high society. However, one encounter proved to be rather exceptional. A letter of introduction from Ralph Waldo Emerson took Henry and his ladies to the home of Jane and Thomas Carlyle, noted writers. Mrs. Carlyle turned out to be a very intelligent woman. She could debate the works of Goethe and Schiller (German poets and playwrights) on an equal footing with her husband, who wrote *The Life of Schiller.* Longfellow was impressed.

Thomas Carlyle and Henry Longfellow had something in common. They were both considered outsiders in the London social scene. Carlyle was a Scotsman and Longfellow was an American. Their treatment as second-class citizens was their bond.

Just before leaving London, Henry contacted an English publisher to reprint his two new volumes of *Outre-Mer*. Longfellow quoted him a price. The printer laughed because he could print the volumes for free once they were mailed to him from America since there were no international copyright laws to protect the author. To keep the printer interested, Longfellow compromised at a much lower figure.

The travelers boarded a ship for Hamburg, Germany, their next stop. From there they switched from coach to steamers to reach Denmark. At that time, they found Denmark dark and depressing. On a ship from Denmark to Gothenburg, Sweden, there was such a bad storm that they had to return to Denmark.

At that point, Mary Longfellow had been fighting a persistent fever since Hamburg and discovered that she was pregnant. Henry bought a carriage that took them to Stockholm, Sweden.

Here they settled down until the end of August and were constantly amazed at the land of the midnight sun when day seemed never to end. Henry was tutored in Swedish by a librarian and found it softer in tone than Danish. He also learned a little Finnish.

Some of his contacts had left Stockholm for the summer, but the American minister to Sweden opened doors for

Longfellow that brought him into the company of other Swedish authors and men of letters. On his own, he traveled to the University of Uppsala to do more research.

With the increasing discomfort of his wife, Longfellow and his ladies returned to Copenhagen, Denmark, which they found more enchanting this time. Henry earnestly studied the Danish language. He dabbled in learning Icelandic, too.

His next mission was to learn the Dutch language. The group of four stayed in Amsterdam for a month because of Mary's ill-health. Briefly they stopped at The Hague. Here Mary Goddard received a letter from her brother, announcing news of her father's death. Her sorrow was so great that Henry arranged for someone to escort her to London and then to a ship, sailing for America. This also meant that Longfellow would have to carry the financial burden for her share of the trip. Clara Crowninshield remained with Henry and Mary Longfellow.

When they reached Rotterdam, Holland, Mary's condition worsened and she had a miscarriage. Henry was distraught. The doctor was not hopeful because of her weakened condition. Despite her decline, Mary remained positive and cheerful to the end.

Clara Crowninshield recounted those final moments in her journal. "She clasped Henry's neck with her almost lifeless arm and said, 'Henry, it is hard to die and leave you. I remember all your kindness to me.' 'You are going to your best friend,' said Henry."

When it was over, Henry kissed her gently and took her rings, placing them on his own fingers. Throughout the night he wept. It was Clara who packed Mary's belongings while Henry arranged for the coffin to be shipped to the Mount Auburn Cemetery in Cambridge.

How would Longfellow deal with his unspeakable grief?

14. Stephen and Zilpah W. Longfellow (parents of Henry).

15. Young Henry Longfellow, watercolor by Ann Hall.

16. Longfellow's eleven grandchildren: The children of Edith L., and
Richard H. Dana III, taken around 1893.
(From L to R) Delia Farley Dana (1889–1989),
Edmund Trowbridge Dana (1886–1981),
Allston Dana (1884–1952), Frances Appleton Dana (1883–1953),
Henry Wadsworth Longfellow Dana (1881–1950), and
Richard Henry Dana IV (1879–1933).

17. Anne L. Thorp and her five daughters;
(Back row L to R) Amelia Chapman Thorp Knowles,
Erica Thorp deBerry, Anne Allerga Longfellow Thorp,
Alice Allerga Thorp
(Front row L to R) Priscilla Alden Thorp Smith,
Anne Longfellow Thorp

18. Henry and Edith Longfellow
on the front stairs of 105 Brattle Street.

19. Longfellow Monument: Dr. Charles W. Eliot, a friend of Longfellow's and president of Harvard from 1869 to 1909, described the 1914 Daniel Chester French memorial as a "... worthy memorial to a famous man, whose life work makes Cambridge a precious place, not only to those who live in it, but to millions who have never set foot within its borders."

CHAPTER SEVEN

"Once, ah, once within these walls"

Recovery and Teaching at Harvard

7. The Vassall-Craigie-Longfellow House was built in 1759 for Major John Vassall. Longfellow lived here from 1837–1882.

Desperately lonely and consumed by sorrow, Longfellow left Rotterdam within a few days of his wife's passing on November 29, 1835. He chaperoned Clara Crowninshield to Heidelberg, Germany, making sightseeing stops at Bonn and other places along the way. When the two travelers reached Heidelberg, they found rooms in separate boarding houses.

The view of the Rhine River from his window and the gardens behind were a great comfort for the grieving widower. There were other professors lodging there, too, giving him diversion and intellectual companionship.

Although Heidelberg was full of celebrations at Christmas time, Henry received news from home that doubled his sorrow. His old friend and brother-in-law, George W. Pierce, had died.

Finally, a letter from Dresden, written by Professor Ticknor, lifted his spirits. Ticknor offered some guidance to Henry for enduring his grief, "I pray God to give you that support without which all external consolation is idle and unavailing. Give yourself to constant and interesting intellectual labor; you will find it will go further than any other human means ..."

Those words of advice gave Longfellow renewed purpose. At the beginning of 1836, he settled down to study German literature. There were some lapses back into grief, which he shared in a letter to his father, "... I feel very lonely and dejected, and the recollection of the last three months of my life overwhelm me with increasing sorrow ... the sense of my bereavement is deep and unutterable."

Heidelberg was a good place for Henry's recovery. The old town was set in the steep and windy Neckar Valley between soaring mountains, which had a soothing effect on his soul. The large, majestic castle, wedged into the mountainside, reminded him of the Alhambra Palace in Spain.

As winter receded, Longfellow felt the need for a spring break. He spent a few days in Frankfurt, Germany, where he saw Goethe's house and attended his favorite Italian opera, *Don Giovanni*.

In June, however, Henry wanted a complete change from Germany. He decided to go to Switzerland. Clara, now captivated by Germany, stayed behind in Heidelberg.

His original plan was to go to Munich, Germany, and then to Florence, Italy, via Milan, to see his good friend George W. Greene before proceeding to Switzerland. But the customs officials at the border of Italy found something wrong with Henry's documents and refused his entry into Italy.

There was no alternative, but to go directly to Switzerland. During July and August, he covered almost every inch of this small country with its dramatic, mountainous landscapes. He found Interlaken, Lake Lucerne, Zurich, and Geneva inspiring. Everything he saw was richly described in his daily journal along with one or two personal confessions, "Every friend seems to keep out of my path; and the world seems lonely."

Finally, Henry met and joined the Motley family from Boston. This companionship was the medicine he needed. In Thun, Switzerland, the Motleys introduced him to the Appletons from Boston. They were on a two year trip around Europe and had just completed the first year. The widowed father, a wealthy textile manufacturer, had brought his two young daughters, Mary and Fanny (Frances), as well as a cousin, William Appleton.

When Henry first presented his card to call on the Appleton family, nineteen-year-old Fanny wrote in her diary that she hoped he wouldn't stay too long, "... though I loved his *Outre-Mer.*" Fanny expected to find an old, boring professor-poet. Upon his arrival, Fanny was surprised to see a young, well-dressed, and handsome man.

The Appletons invited Henry to travel in their company. This interlude of being with attractive young people and discussing poetic works and German ballads, restored in him a sense of fun and family, which he hadn't felt for seven or eight months.

The details of the beginnings of a romance with Fanny Appleton were unclear, but there seemed to be a definite attraction on Henry's part. Fanny had lost her mother in 1833 and her brother Charles in 1834. Perhaps Henry and Fanny were drawn to each other because of losing people for whom they cared deeply.

The bliss that Henry felt in these newfound friendships was shattered when he had a sharp letter from Clara, demanding that Henry return to Heidelberg and chaperone her home in a ship across the Atlantic. Longfellow made plans to depart immediately. He also had to take up his duties at Harvard. The only emotion Fanny showed was in her diary, "I miss Mr. L."

Before sailing back to America, Longfellow revisited Madame Potel's lodgings in Paris. He found them exactly the same. The wide boulevards that he had walked nine years before were still enchanting, but the joys he had experienced in 1826 were somewhat dulled by his personal loss.

By December of 1836, Henry Longfellow arrived in Cambridge, Massachusetts, to prepare for teaching at Harvard College. He began searching for rooms to rent and found a third-story place in Dr. Stearns' home on Professors' Row on Kirkland Street. On the second floor was Cornelius C. Felton, a professor of Greek, whom he befriended. In the future, Felton would become president of Harvard.

These two companions expanded their group of friends to include three other professors. They nicknamed themselves—The Five of Clubs. Besides Longfellow and Felton were Charles Sumner (law professor and a future politician), George Hillard (Sumner's law partner), and Henry R. Cleveland (who lived outside Boston).

In those days, men gravitated to other men for friendship and intellectual gymnastics. Most women were too busy raising children and taking care of the home or entertaining for their husbands. The opinions and viewpoints of women were not always accepted or valued in the public arena, but in private or behind the scenes, women made their ideas known.

Although a desirable guest in Cambridge and Boston societies, Henry's love of colorful clothes drew much criticism from conservative Bostonians. His desire for bright outfits first started in Paris in 1826 and never left him. But people liked his personality so much that they overlooked his strange choices in clothing.

In the world at large between the years of 1837 and 1848, momentous events were happening. German lawyer and philosopher, Karl Marx, collaborated with Frederich Engels in writing articles about the poor conditions of factory workers in 1844. By 1848, they wrote the *Communist Manifesto*, praising socialism and communism as a national way of life. Charles Darwin was also recognized as an outstanding naturalist, publishing two classic books on geology. The Six Year Depression in America from 1837 to 1843 caused treasury notes to be issued, and a bank bill was passed to establish a national bank.

However, this period was a busy one for Longfellow. He befriended the shy and reclusive writer, Nathaniel Hawthorne, when his book *Twice Told Tales* was published. Henry wrote a very positive review of it for the *North American Review*. Naturally, Hawthorne was more than grateful and confessed that he remembered Longfellow's reading of a poem in 1825 at Bowdoin and was greatly impressed.

In a letter to his father, Henry listed the courses that he would be teaching at Harvard: History of the French Language; Languages from South of Europe; History of Gothic Languages; Anglo-Saxon Literature; Swedish Literature; German Literature and Writings of Goethe; and the Life and Writings of Jean Paul Richter (a German writer of prose).

It was a huge workload—much greater than his courses taught at Bowdoin. Longfellow wrote President Quincy to ask permission to reduce his teaching schedule. No reply was forthcoming until August when they agreed to lighten his teaching load in small ways.

After having spent so much time in hotels and boarding houses, Henry missed the home atmosphere that he enjoyed as a married man with Mary. Thus, he began searching for different accommodations in May of 1837.

A law student friend, McLane, had taken rooms at the Craigie House at 105 Brattle Street in Cambridge, but he was soon moving out. Brattle Street was within walking distance to Harvard Square (known as the Cambridge Village) and Harvard College.

One beautiful May day, Henry walked down wealthy "Tory Row," as Brattle Street had been called in the 1700s. He stopped at the large Craigie House to say goodbye to McLane, who introduced him to Mrs. Craigie. When he asked about renting rooms, she quickly told him that she did not want to rent to any more students. Before she totally dismissed him, he informed her that he was a professor at Harvard and the author of *Outre-Mer.*

Mrs. Craigie's attitude completely changed. She had a copy of Henry's book on her table. Still in disbelief, she invited him to see her copy. Since she had a complete collection of the works of the French writer Voltaire in her library, one might imagine that the two conversed in French.

Charmed by young Longfellow, she gave him a tour and historical background of the whole house. The original house was built in 1759 by Major John Vassall, who was pro-British during the Revolutionary War. Once his views were known, the family was forced to leave the house and escape to Boston.

Soon Glover's Marblehead Regiment moved into the house. Not long afterwards, General George Washington made his Revolutionary War headquarters there from July 1775 to April 1776.

Mrs. Craigie proudly showed Henry the two front rooms on the second floor that Washington occupied. One was for sleeping and one served as an office/study. Because Henry had heard so much about this period in history from his grandfather, Peleg Wadsworth, he was doubly interested. At this point, the landlady offered the two front rooms to Longfellow. He was ecstatic and accepted.

Longfellow would always be in awe of General George Washington's presence in the Craigie House and its historic value. In 1876, Longfellow wrote a poem, *To a Child*, that would show what the General faced during his months at his Revolutionary War headquarters in Cambridge. Here is stanza six from that poem:

> *Once, ah, once within these walls,*
> *One whom memory oft recalls,*
> *The Father of his Country, dwelt.*
> *And yonder meadows broad and damp*
> *The fires of the besieging camp*
> *Encircled with a burning belt.*
> *Up and down these echoing stairs,*
> *Heavy with the weight of cares,*
> *Sounded his majestic tread;*
> *Yes, within this very room*
> *Sat he in those hours of gloom,*
> *Weary both in heart and head.*

Mrs. Craigie seemed pleased with her new tenant and said that Miriam would serve breakfast in his rooms each morning at a small price (the price wasn't so small!) and dinner if he wished. Henry often walked from Cambridge to Boston to eat dinner there and strolled across the Boston Common before returning home.

Andrew Craigie, Mrs. Craigie's late husband, had bought the house in 1791. Not only was he a wealthy landowner, but he had been Apothecary General to the American Army. He loved the situation of the house, surrounded by 140 acres, sliding down to the Charles River with an unobstructed view. His desire was to enlarge the house, but to preserve the many historic aspects related to George Washington. This was a costly venture. Andrew Craigie died when the work was completed, leaving his wife with very little money. Therefore, his widow began to rent rooms as a means of support.

Once his living quarters were established, Henry devoted most of his time to teaching. Without qualified assistants, much of the administrative duties fell to him, leaving very little creative time for writing his own poetry. Also, the classical department of Greek and Latin at Harvard was still considered more respected than modern languages.

Nevertheless, Henry made two major contributions to the method of teaching. One was to address each student formally as "Mr." and the other was to introduce certain cultural aspects of the country and not just the language itself. Often he would take an author from the specific country, give a little biographical background, and read something from his work.

Professor Longfellow had a definite style of teaching. His students never knew what to expect. He kept their attention through his unconventional dress and by his theatrical presentation. Like a Shakespearian actor, he brought his subjects to life.

Despite his circulation in society and the comradeship of his colleagues, Longfellow was still battling depression over the loss of his wife.

Would he ever write poetry again and would he ever find love again?

CHAPTER EIGHT

"Friends my soul with you remembers!"

Cambridge Colleagues and Creativity

8. H.W. Longfellow by S. Laurence, 1845.

The "Five of Clubs" frequently visited Henry at the Craigie House. Professor Felton came more often than the others. The men talked of many things such as literature and politics. Charles Sumner was very emotional and would flare up over the topic of slavery. His anti-slavery views offended many outsiders, but not the group of five.

From 1837 to 1845, Henry Longfellow often sat in the upstairs corner of his study and began to use his quill pen again to create short and long poems. It was the start of a renewed creative period.

In 1837, *Flowers* was the first poem that moved him forward. Although some friends criticized it, Longfellow was satisfied. When the *Knickerbocker Magazine* published it, the title was changed to *Floral Astrology*. Curiously, the poem recalled the flowers along the Rhine River in Germany rather than the flowers outside his window near the Charles River.

> *One who dwelleth by the castled Rhine,*
> *When he called the flowers, so blue and golden.*

One of Longfellow's most memorable poems was written in July of 1838. It was called *A Psalm of Life* and was widely praised. With only nine verses, it was often memorized and quoted; especially the following verse.

Lives of great men all remind us
We can make our lives sublime,
And, departing, leave behind us
Footprints on the sands of time;.

Perhaps, Longfellow was referring to Goethe or to himself or to mankind.

In his classes, Henry would discuss the lives of famous literary men. He lectured on Goethe's *Faust*, a long play in which Faust makes a pact with the devil. Much later *Faust* was translated into a popular opera. Another favorite of Longfellow's was the 13th and 14th century Italian author, Dante Alighieri, who wrote *The Divine Comedy*. The story revolves around the main character, Dante Pilgrim, who goes on a three day trip through the Inferno, Purgatory, and Paradise. In the future, Dante's work would absorb Henry's time. But for now, he would use and discuss the work in his lectures.

Henry's life seemed to be full. He was creating, reading, teaching, and venturing beyond the walls of Craigie House. Sometimes he would go to Boston to see a production of Shakespeare's play *King Lear* or hear a lecture by Ralph Waldo Emerson—one of the famous Transcendentalists from Concord, Massachusetts. Transcendentalists were a circle of literary men and women from the Boston area in the 1840s. They wanted to transcend material knowledge and to explore an ideal spiritual reality.

In the summer of 1838, Henry had wanted to give lectures at the college chapel and make them open to the public. However, the Harvard Corporation discouraged that idea. Henry commented on their decision in his journal, "Human life is made up mostly of a series of little disappointments and little pleasures."

A letter to Charles Sumner noted that most of their Five of Clubs members were getting married. Henry told Sumner, "I am lonely."

Although still guilt-ridden over the death of his wife, Henry had a secret longing for Fanny Appleton's companionship. When the Appleton family returned from Europe in 1837, Henry had called on them at 39 Beacon Street— one of the large and elegant townhouses on the slope overlooking Boston Common. He apparently revealed his heart to her and was rejected, but the flame inside him wouldn't go out. On his many walking trips to Boston from Cambridge, he may have hoped to catch a glimpse of her. His strolls through the Boston Common may have been intended to watch her house, hoping to see her figure go in or out. He was a heartsick lover and flung himself into work to forget his personal pain. Fanny had a teasing way of making fun of him and called him the "prof."

After the September graduation exercises at Harvard in 1838, Longfellow seemed to fall in and out of depression. He wrote to his father, "Dejected,—no sunshine in the soul. Cannot bring my mind to work." In a moment of honesty, he also confided to his father about the unpleasant part of teaching, "Perhaps the worst thing in a college life is this having your mind constantly a playmate for boys—constantly adapting itself to them instead of stretching out and grappling with men's minds."

Despite these moody references, Longfellow recorded in his journal that he had taken notes and was preparing to start writing a long travel novel called *Hyperion*. In Greek mythology, Hyperion was a giant sun god.

The charms of the 1838 autumn seemed to inspire him anew. While at Harvard, he started teaching Spanish drama, which contributed to his high spirits. His October journal revealed his work ethic, "Worked at *Hyperion* again. Wrote chapter six of Book IV, a touch of philosophical dreamery. But I have so many interruptions!"

When time allowed, Henry traveled to Nahant, a resort town north of Boston near Lynn. The causeway was like the spindly leg of a baby ostrich with its body perched atop the hip and its beak pointed north to Maine. The spit of land was sandy and filled with tall, eerie-looking fossil rocks, jutting into the sky and anchored in the water at the very root. At sunset, Longfellow used to watch a herd of cows, marching across the beach and casting their lumpy shadows on the shoreline as they headed home to Lynn.

During the winter vacation of 1839, he even ventured to New York City to lecture and to visit writers. From there he pushed south to Washington, D.C. and spent fifteen minutes with President Van Buren, discussing mundane topics such as the weather. Sometimes, Henry returned to

Portland to renew his childhood recollections. In a fleeting moment, he considered starting a newspaper with friends. This never materialized.

However, *Hyperion* did materialize in print during the summer of 1839. The major part of the poetic prose was to introduce German literature, but the minor part was a sensational love story that caught the interest of everyone, insuring many sales. It was the romantic encounter in Switzerland between Paul Flemming (Longfellow) and Mary Ashburton (Fanny). Every detail of his own travelogue in 1836 was described. The plot—to those who knew the unhappy love story—was very transparent.

Henry sent a copy to the Appleton family, and Fanny was not pleased. She distanced herself even further from Henry. In her own journal, she made a few unpleasant remarks about Longfellow's work.

Longfellow's first volume of *Voices of the Night* was published in December of 1839. Immediately, he began work on volume two. Often his nights of sleep were restless because his ideas would come in the darkness and he would leap out of bed to write them down.

In 1840 Longfellow was concerned about the publishing industry. Financially, many publishers were on the verge of bankruptcy. Henry had not been paid in three years for articles or books. His publisher of *Hyperion* had been hounded by bill collectors, and Longfellow's books were seized, but eventually released.

These circumstances did not stop Henry's creative flow. He ventured into the ballad form of his poetry and wrote *The Wreck of the Hesperus*, which described the actual shipwreck of a schooner near the Gloucester, Massachusetts, harbor. He hoped to get it published first in a newspaper.

By 1839 another famous poem of Longfellow's would find its way into print. Every day when Henry walked to Harvard along Brattle Street, he would pass the village blacksmith, Dexter Pratt. Stephen Longfellow, his great, great grandfather, had been a hardworking blacksmith. The Cambridge blacksmith reminded him of the strength and endurance needed by a smithy. Longfellow wrote *The Village Blacksmith* in honor of his ancestor.

> *Under a spreading chestnut-tree*
> *The village smithy stands;*
> *The smith, a mighty man is he,*
> *With large and sinewy hands;*
> *And the muscles of his brawny arms*
> *Are strong as iron bands.*

When writing a letter to George Greene, Henry told him how he felt about criticism of his work. "I understand there is a spicy article against me in the Boston Quarterly. I shall get it as soon as I can; for strange as you may think it, these things give me no pain." This remark shows Longfellow's confidence in his own work.

In the same letter to Greene, Henry offered advice to a writer starting a new work. "I have great faith in not saying much about a thing until you can say, I have done it."

For Longfellow, January of 1840 was devoted to reading Dante's *Inferno* because he would be going to New York to give a lecture on Dante. Other famous writers, such as Emerson, would also be lecturing on different topics.

Life in the spring of 1840 was full of the twelve lectures on Dante and Spanish drama that Longfellow would deliver to his students. In the evenings, he would dine with his friends from the Five of Clubs.

In December of that year, his third edition of *Voices of the Night* would be published and the fifth edition by the following spring. However in that same December of 1840, Henry fulfilled his long desire of writing a play. This would be *The Spanish Student* in five acts. He was not ready to have it published until 1843, which gave him time to polish and revise it. Knowing his passion for Spain and Spanish women, it was no surprise that a lively Spanish gypsy girl featured in his play as an exotic dancer who offends the clergy. Not considered stage-worthy, Longfellow's only play had one performance in German in 1855.

Feeling very much in the doldrums in 1842, Longfellow needed a change. The routine and monotony of teaching had plunged him into a depression.

Despite his gloom, Longfellow was cheered by the visit of British author, Charles Dickens. In his daily journal, Henry described him thus, "He is a gay, free, and easy character; with a fine bright face, blue eyes, and long dark hair." When Dickens and Longfellow attended a theatrical performance in Boston, Dickens was introduced to a wild reception of nine cheers. He had to stand and take a bow before the show could begin.

Charles Sumner and Longfellow appointed themselves tour guides of historic Boston for Dickens. They took him to Copps Hill, where signal lanterns were placed in the steeple of the Old North Church. They also showed him the 221 foot granite monument at Bunker Hill, where the colonists were defeated in a fierce battle of the American Revolution. Before Dickens set out on his American lecture tour, Longfellow hosted a breakfast for him at Craigie House with Professor Felton and Andrews Norton (a Harvard professor and Biblical scholar) as guests.

After Dickens returned to England, he wrote a letter to Longfellow, inviting him to visit in London and almost demanding that Henry stay with him.

To improve his physical and mental health, Henry asked Harvard for a six month leave of absence to take the "water cure" in Germany. Maybe he was seeking the cure of a broken heart. Fanny Appleton had dangled him for six years and toyed with his affections to the breaking point.

Therefore, in April of 1842, Longfellow set sail for his beloved Europe from New York. Once there, he stopped in Paris to renew old acquaintances and to fill his mind with precious memories and familiar sights.

Then, Henry made his way to the Rhine River after passing through Belgium. Once aboard the steamer, Longfellow brooded over writing a poem about the history of Jesus Christ, which he would title *Christus*.

Longfellow intended to spend the summer at Marienberg, Germany, situated on a green bluff, overlooking a garden of blue flowers. This was an old nunnery, converted into rooms for guests, taking the water cure. Henry especially loved the peace and quiet. In his journal, there was a hint that he might have had a flirtation with a beautiful German lady.

There was a daily routine of taking six baths a day, alternating between cold and hot. The meals were very Spartan, but there were many long walks throughout the day.

In a letter to his father, Longfellow confessed, "Home is pleasanter than this wandering alone over the world." Could he have been homesick? He remarked that he still did not feel restored to perfect health.

The one bright spot was a lifelong friendship he formed with German poet Ferdinand Freiligrath. They formed a mutual admiration society in exchanging and appreciating each other's work.

By mid-September, Longfellow prepared to leave the spa. There had been many colorful characters at the nunnery during his stay. His journal noted, "For it is one of my weaknesses to become attached to people and places."

From Germany, Henry headed to London to accept Dickens' invitation to stay with him. Charles was eager to introduce him to the literary society of London. Dickens had just published a book about his American trip, called *American Notes*, in which he praised much about America, but also criticized the problem of slavery.

By mid-October, Longfellow was ready to go home. Aboard ship, he started writing poems about American slavery—probably inspired by Dickens. Henry's father influenced him as well. Stephen Longfellow had long opposed slavery and had books in his library about emancipation.

This excerpt from the poem *The Witnesses* revealed Henry's boldness on the subject of slavery.

> *All evil thoughts and deeds;*
> *anger, and lust, and pride;*
> *The foulest, rankest weeds,*
> *That choke Life's groaning tide!*
>
> *These are the woes of Slaves;*
> *They glare from the abyss;*
> *They cry, from unknown graves,*
> *"We are the Witnesses!"*

Longfellow was happy to be home. After seven years of yearning for Fanny Appleton's love, would she ever relent and accept his affections?

CHAPTER NINE

"Love, love, what wilt thou with this heart of mine?"

Second Love, Family, and Success

9. Frances (Fanny) Appleton Longfellow, "crayon" drawing by S. Rowse.

It happened at an April party in Boston where Henry and Fanny were both invited. Fanny hadn't seen Longfellow in a year because of his travels abroad and probably because he had given up all hope. At the party, she indicated that she might like to see him again.

What made her soften? There could be a number of factors. One, her sister had married and moved away. Two, her father had remarried a younger woman—about Fanny's age. Three, there didn't seem to be any suitors on the horizon. Not to be married in those days at the age of twenty-six for a young woman usually meant a life of spinsterhood. Another reason for his lack of acceptability to the Appletons was the fact that Henry came from Portland and didn't have a high enough position in society. However, his increasing fame in America and in Europe as a poet and a Harvard professor changed that attitude.

Fanny's journal told us what she said to Henry at that party, "You must come and comfort me, Mr. Longfellow." There was correspondence back and forth between them. Maybe she had forgiven him for his mockery of her in *Hyperion*, and she realized that his grief over his first wife's death was finally over.

After receiving a note from Henry, she replied, "I have just received your note and I cannot forbear telling you that it has comforted me greatly ... I should never have ventured to speak so frankly to you had I not believed the dead Past had buried its dead and that we might safely walk over their graves, thanking God that at last we could live to give each other only happy thoughts."

Probably in Henry's reply, he proposed to her and she accepted on May 10, 1843. His joy was so unbounded that he walked briskly from Craigie House to 39 Beacon Street to greet his true love—now his bride-to-be.

After their engagement was official, Fanny wrote letters to Henry's sister Anne and to his parents. This is what she wrote to her future mother-in-law, Zilpah Longfellow: "Would that language could reveal to you how fully I appreciate the priceless blessing God has vouchsafed me in your son's affection, and how fervently I pray to become worthy of it, and to improve my character through his.... Heart to heart I trust you will always permit me, and will learn to love one who offers you a daughter's fond respect." Fanny had been without a mother since a teenager and may have longed for a mother's love, which she hoped to find in Zilpah.

The wedding took place on July 13, 1843 at Fanny's home. She wore a white muslin dress with touches of orange blossoms tied to her hair and threaded along the sides of her dress. That evening, the happy bride and groom returned by carriage under a glowing moon to Craigie House.

Fanny's sensitive attitude toward *Hyperion* had changed by the time of their engagement. In fact, Fanny displayed a sense of humor by the wedding gift that she gave Henry. It was her sketch book from Switzerland during the time they first met. She inscribed it "To Paul Flemming, from Mary Ashburton."

Mrs. Craigie had passed away, and Henry was now renting the eastern half of the house through the Craigie estate. Eager to own the entire house, Fanny told her father of the circumstances, and he purchased it for them in October of 1843 for ten thousand dollars. It would be considered a wedding present to the newlyweds. For a time, they continued to rent out the western part of the house until their family expanded.

Fanny embarked on a redecorating spree in which she preferred European textiles to American. This decision offended her father, whose life was spent producing American fabrics and carpets from his Lowell, Massachusetts, factory. She promised him that after her initial plan, she would always buy American.

Because Fanny and Henry had traveled extensively in Europe as young people, they had a great appreciation for preserving historic buildings and artifacts. Therefore, they both agreed to save and preserve the historic memorabilia, related to George Washington's nine month stay in their house. The Craigie House was also known as General Washington's Headquarters until many decades later. Then it became more strongly associated with Longfellow.

Marriage to his wonderful second love agreed with Henry. The couple started a family rather quickly with their firstborn son, Charles, in June of 1844. The other five children arrived in this order: Ernest Wadsworth (1845),

Frances (1847, but who died in 1848), Alice Mary (1850), Edith (1853), and Anne Allegra (1855).

With this growing family, the Longfellows sought relief from the hot, steamy summers in Cambridge. They tried different places such as Vermont, the Berkshires and Nahant in Massachusetts, Rhode Island, and Portland, Maine. They spent a long summer at the Verandah Hotel, overlooking Casco Bay in Maine. The sights and sounds impacted his poetry, describing the Maine coastline. Here he wrote, *The Tides Rises, the Tide Falls*, recorded earlier in this book.

Once Henry settled into family life, his professional writing career blossomed. His volumes of poetry were prospering in the marketplace. A new volume, *The Belfry of Bruges*, resulted from his visit to Belgium during his last visit to Europe. *The Bridge* poem, although supposedly in Belgium, was actually located in Boston where he walked across the Charles River during a period of great despair. Here are a few verses that reveal his inner pain:

> *How often, oh how often,*
> *In the days that had gone by,*
> *I had stood on that bridge at midnight*
> *And gazed on that wave and sky!*
>
> *How often, oh how often,*
> *I had wished that the ebbing tide*
> *Would bear me away on its bosom*
> *O'er the ocean wild and wide!*

For my heart was hot and restless,
And my life was full of care,
And the burden laid upon me
Seemed greater than I could bear.

With praise from many readers also came criticism from other writers such as author Edgar Allen Poe, a Southerner who resented Longfellow's poems on slavery. Margaret Fuller, a reviewer for "The New York Tribune," was very harsh in her criticism of Longfellow's work. One could assume that professional jealousy may have been a factor as well as racial prejudice on Poe's part.

Sometimes authors file away ideas in their minds or on paper until they resurface at the proper time. Such was the case with one of Longfellow's most famous epic poems, *Evangeline*, which he extracted from his memory in 1846.

The idea first came to him at a dinner party at his house when Nathaniel Hawthorne brought an Episcopal priest from Salem with him. Over dinner, the clergyman related an allegedly true story that he had heard from a French Canadian woman.

The story went something like this. On the day of their wedding, a young couple from Acadia (a section of central Nova Scotia near Halifax) had been separated by an invasion of British troops that were forcing out the French population who had moved there many years before from the western shore of Nova Scotia. This forced deportation was in 1755. The lovers searched for each other for twenty years. Not until her lover was on his deathbed did the woman find him and hold him in her arms as he took his dying breath.

Longfellow was enchanted by the story and by the dedication and loyalty of the young woman to keep searching for her missing husband-to-be. Henry asked Hawthorne if he wanted to turn the idea into a novel. Hawthorne shook his head in the negative. At which point, Longfellow asked if Hawthorne would mind if he used it in poetic form. Again, Hawthorne expressed his disinterest. After the party was over, Hawthorne wished that he had not dismissed the idea, but it was too late.

In 1845, Longfellow began work on this idea. He took the basic plot, but enlarged and fictionalized it. Henry made up the mythical name of Grand Pre, Nova Scotia, from where they were exiled. Instead of searching for each other only in New England, Longfellow had the leading character, Evangeline, go to the swamps of Louisiana (where they speak French), looking for her beloved, Gabriel. Longfellow created drama and suspense when the lovers pass each other like ships in the night without knowing it. Not until Evangeline finds Gabriel on his deathbed in Philadelphia are the two reunited. He dies and when she dies shortly thereafter, they are buried together—united in death. Longfellow adopted the basic technique used in playwriting: boy meets girl, but boy doesn't get girl until the end of the play or the novel.

Henry put *Evangeline* into hexameter verse, but without rhymes. It became a popular long epic poem for his public. He was working on the final proofs at the Verandah Hotel in Maine in September of 1847.

By the summer of 1848, *Evangeline* was so popular that it went into its sixth printing. Despite its popularity, the press critics called the character of Evangeline "a goody goody" and they didn't like the hexameter style. Nathaniel Hawthorne came to Longfellow's defense in a newspaper interview, giving the poet credit for its poetic beauty. Others in Great Britain and America found it inspiring. Longfellow didn't mind because the poem was selling and he felt positive about it.

Fanny also was thrilled with its reception. She wrote to a relative, "I suppose I can now tell you that he is correcting the proofs of a long poem called *Evangeline*, written in hexameters, describing the fortunes and misfortunes of an Acadian damsel driven to this country from Canada by the British in the olden time. It is a very beautiful, touching poem."

Unfortunately, the infant death of his first daughter, Frances, in 1848 was a great pain to him. He wrote about it in a collection of poems called *The Seaside and The Fireside*. The one about Frances was a short poem, *Resignation*. Because men in that period did not reveal their deepest feelings, Longfellow was criticized for it, but his words of grief touched the hearts of many. These are the final two verses of *Resignation:*

And though at times impetuous with emotion
And anguish long suppressed,
The swelling heart heaves moaning like the ocean,
That cannot be at rest,—

We will be patient, and assuage the feeling
We may not wholly stay;
By silence sanctifying, not concealing,
The grief that must have way.

The little family brought Henry Longfellow his greatest joy and happiness. He loved being a husband and a father. Unlike most fathers of that period, he was not a strict disciplinarian. Fanny did some disciplining, but she, too, tried to reason with rather than to spank her children.

Fanny, a devoted Unitarian, was anxious to begin the spiritual education of her children. When Charley was four-years-old, she wrote in her journal on October 11, 1847, "I spoke to him for the first time of loving and obeying another being than his earthly parents ... Upon this happy impulse I called him to me and told him, with reverent manner, he had another papa up in the sky ... His dark eyes dilated with childish wonder and interest and he said at once, 'I want to go up there and see him. I want to take Erny up there to see him.'"

Henry enjoyed playing with Charley. The two of them would fly kites outside on the meadow and catch the winds coming off the Charles River. Instead of pulling out dandelions in the lawn, Charley would hammer them into the grass while his father laughed and helped him. While Henry was away teaching at Harvard, little Charley would look everywhere and cry sadly, "Where's Papa?"

Both Charley and Erny were very active children—not unlike their father's toddler years. However, Erny would often have a tantrum. Henry would quietly wait until the tantrum was over and then would fold Erny into his arms, kissing and calming him. One time Erny said to his father, "Help me, help me, I don't want to be like that."

The three Longfellow daughters had distinct personalities, too. Alice Mary loved to read stories from the books on the parlor table and made her parents laugh by her amusing statements. At Nahant, she played fairyland among the rocks. Edith, though angelic looking, had a stubborn and willful attitude. Anne Allegra paraded up and down the Nahant beaches until the wandering cows chased her away.

Every night at Craigie House, the small Longfellow children couldn't wait to say goodnight to their father. When he was finished with his working day, the old grandfather clock on the landing of the front stairs would strike and chime for seven minutes. In their nightdresses and pajamas, they would whisper at the bottom of the stairs and then ambush their father in his study, climbing over him and kissing him. This ritual inspired his well-known poem of 1859, *The Children's Hour.*

Between the dark and the daylight,
When the night is beginning to lower,
Comes a pause in the day's occupations,
That is known as the Children's Hour.

Henry was saddened when the children started to school. He loved reading them stories from Grimm's *Fairy Tales* or making up his own. Charley was full of adventure and Erny loved to sketch.

There were two other events that brought Henry Longfellow great sorrow. His father passed away in the summer of 1849 and his mother in the summer of 1851. He and his father had become very close over the years and there was a frequent exchange of letters. Henry often used his father as his confidante and enjoyed literary exchanges with his mother.

But the successful poet had another dream to fulfill. What was it?

CHAPTER TEN

"Come to me, O ye children! For I hear you at your play"

His Dream and Great Loss

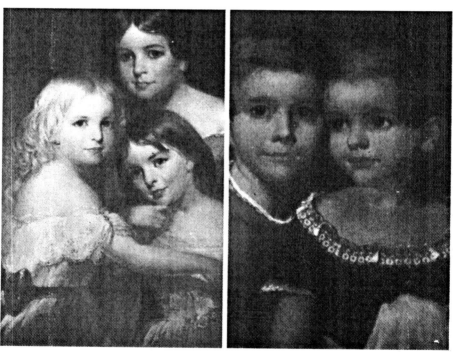

10. Alice, Edith, and Anne Longfellow 11. Charles and Ernest Longfellow
By T. B. Read. By Eastman Johnson.

Longfellow was riding a wave of success in the 1850s.

He turned to prose with an allegory for a comic novel, called *Kavanagh*, which describes different characters, set in the Berkshires of western Massachusetts. Mr. Churchill is the leading commentator. Arthur Kavanagh, a minister, is looking for romance, but he can't decide between two ladies. Longfellow's real purpose of the book, however, was to show that culture and literature were not confined to American shores, but were influenced by great art from Europe.

As rumblings about slavery grew to a higher pitch in the 1850s, Longfellow found his political views in line with the new Republican Party. Because the Party was against slavery, Charles Sumner and Henry joined. In fact, Sumner was elected to the U.S. Senate. With Abraham Lincoln's election in 1860, Longfellow was convinced that the country would be unified over the slavery issue. For years, Fanny's letters to friends and family were filled with her own commentaries on the impending Civil War. In February 25, 1861, she wrote, "… Mr. Lincoln has reached Washington safely, and we hope soon to feel his firm hand on the helm."

Between 1843 and 1854, Longfellow devoted as much time to his home life as his teaching schedule and writing commitments would allow. Henry was enlarging his book collection—his passion and delight—which would reach 14,000 books, including Shakespeare, Dante, 75 volumes of France's Voltaire, Spain's Miguel de Cervantes, Swiss-born

Louis Agassiz, American abolitionists—Samuel and Julia Ward (father and daughter) as well as works in Greek, German, French, Swedish, and Finnish.

Both Fanny and Henry loved art and accumulated 4,500 artifacts from around the world. These included paintings from France and sculptures of Homer, Schiller, and Goethe by renowned artists. They bought furniture in the 18th century Queen Anne and Chippendale styles. The wallpaper was in the 1840s Decorative Arts style. Their son Charley contributed furniture, porcelain, and paintings from China and Japan where he traveled as a grown man. Charley's love of Asian art was contagious among Bostonians, who began purchasing oriental art and furniture.

During the 1840s and 1850s, they also had portraits made of themselves and their children. Eastman Johnson, a well-known portrait artist from Maine, did a pastel of young Charley and Erny. He made a charcoal portrait of Longfellow as well as many of Henry's close friends. There is a familiar oil painting of the three girls in the dining room by Thomas Buchan Read of "Grave Alice, and laughing Allegra, and Edith with golden hair" (two lines from *The Children's Hour*). There is an enchanting painting of Fanny by G. P. A. Healy next to the portrait of the girls and elsewhere another one of her in a crayon drawing by Samuel W. Rowse. In the front parlor there is a marble bust of Fanny by Lorenzo Bartolini.

In her diary, Fanny admitted that she loved the summers in Nahant and other places because the family was together.

But her thoughts of being a housewife in Cambridge until 1854 were these, "… in a week we return to Cambridge, which *entre nous* [between us], has become, outside my own house, a dreary place to me, so few intimate friends have I there, so monotonous is my life."

Henry's own personal monotony was soon to change. Since his days as a professor at Bowdoin, Longfellow had yearned for the time when he could give up teaching to spend his days in his own study within the walls of his own home to create.

Celebrity status had brought wealth to Longfellow. His poetry and prose were bestsellers—some selling as many as 50,000 copies. He had become a superstar in the world of literature both in America and other countries.

The year 1854 was a key landmark for Henry Longfellow. After 18 years of teaching modern languages and comparative literature at Harvard, Henry resigned from his duties at the College and turned fulltime to his long-held dream of working at home.

His first project focused on Indians. Since childhood and throughout his college years, Longfellow had been fascinated by Native American Indians, especially in Maine. The Wabanaki tribe in Maine had dwindled down to a few hundred at the time of Henry's youth. In fact his first published piece of writing at thirteen had been about the battle at Lovell's Pond between the Indians and an American captain.

Once Henry established his work schedule at home, he embarked on a long epic poem, entitled *The Song of Hiawatha*. Despite common prejudice against Native Americans from many intellectuals, Longfellow began his research in the Harvard Library. He patterned *Hiawatha* after a Finnish epic, which used a primitive meter—just what Longfellow wanted for this poem. It would sound like the beat of a drum when read aloud.

In the poem, Hiawatha was a mythical Indian chief, who lived in the land of the Ojibway Indians near Lake Superior in Minnesota. Longfellow's purpose in writing the poem was to bring out the traditions and special qualities of the Indians before they became a vanishing race.

Ye who love a nation's legends,
Love the ballads of a people
That like voices from afar off
Call to us to pause and listen.

Composer Antonin Dvorak used the Hiawatha poem for his Ninth or "New World" Symphony, composed in 1892.

Longfellow continued to work on *Hiawatha*, writing 22 cantos (like chapters in a book) while his young family played in the surf on the beaches of Nahant, where they rented a cottage in the summer of 1854. By the spring of 1855, he had almost finished *Hiawatha*. At a hotel in Newport, Rhode Island, in the summer, he had put the finishing touches on it for his publisher, who gave him

$1,000 in October for the first edition of a 5,000 copy print run in November.

Like a John Grisham novel of today, the public couldn't wait for another long poem by Henry Longfellow. *The Song of Hiawatha* was well received. Ralph Waldo Emerson called it a "Wholesome" poem. Each canto dealt with a certain aspect of Indian life or its culture. Some critics called it too heavy—almost like a German opera. Whatever the drawbacks, the character of Hiawatha wanted to unite his people in peace. He wanted them to be strong to combat the invasion by the white man. As the white man encroached on Indian land, Hiawatha moved westward.

Despite the fickleness of critics and the public, Longfellow ignored them and enjoyed his life with his family. Life was ideal. In summers they were at the seashore and in winters they would bring out the big sleigh from the carriage house behind their home. The horses would be harnessed and away they would go on the roads of Cambridge after a snowstorm. The children loved it as did Henry and Fanny.

In 1858 Longfellow focused on his Pilgrim ancestry, going back on his mother's side to John and Priscilla Alden. This resulted in his popular poem *The Courtship of Miles Standish*. The story begins with John Alden in love with Priscilla Mullins, but he feels inadequate and without confidence in pursuing her. Before he can find the courage to woo her, his closest friend, the blustering Captain Miles Standish, comes to John to ask him to go to Priscilla and propose marriage to her for him. John agrees to carry out the mission for the Captain. When John Alden confronts Priscilla with Standish's marriage proposal, Priscilla totally rejects the idea. The words of her response have become a famous quote. She said, "Why don't you speak for yourself, John?" The inevitable happens. John woos, wins, and marries Priscilla, leaving Miles Standish as the rejected lover. This plot is similar to the French play, *Cyrano de Bergerac*, performed in Paris in 1897. Longfellow's *The Courtship of Miles Standish* sold 25,000 copies in two months.

Fanny, too, found her life to be idyllic in 1858. She wrote in her diary, "As I grow older I think I enjoy more and more my shell, like one of Mr. Agassiz's venerable turtles, whose physiognomies are so accurately painted in his wonderful great book, and I find it very hard to emerge from it for the attractions of other people's. We very rarely ... go out of an evening, we so dearly delight in our own fireside, and the boys utter such a lament if we do that I have not the heart to cut them off from their nightly readings."

For years, Fanny's brother, Thomas Appleton, and Henry had been trying to purchase a cottage at Nahant for sharing. Finally, in 1860 they found one and shared the cost. Also in 1860, Longfellow had a poem published in the *Atlantic Monthly* magazine. It was titled *Paul Revere's Ride*. This poem would remain famous for generations. These opening lines are well-known to American children and adults even today.

Listen my children, and you shall hear
Of the midnight ride of Paul Revere,
On the eighteenth of April, in Seventy-five;
Hardly a man is now alive
Who remembers that famous day and year.

To all appearances in 1861, Henry Wadsworth Longfellow had everything—wealth, fame, and a happy family. He was fifty-four-years old and in the prime of life. However, his country was still divided over the slavery issue and the Civil War was on the horizon.

In July of 1861, he would experience the greatest tragedy of his life since the loss of his first wife in 1835. It began when Fanny was in the library with two of their three daughters while Henry was sleeping in his study.

This July day was very hot. Fanny decided to cut locks from the hair of Anne and Edith and seal them with wax in packets to save as keepsakes. Anne was playing with matches on the floor when her mother leaned down to pick them up and put them back in their box. As she did so, her shoe stepped on the heads of the matches, which struck a flame. Within seconds, her muslin dress caught fire. Fanny rushed into the study and awakened Henry. Stunned, he grabbed a small hearth rug and tried to smother the flames while holding her. She rushed from his arms back to the hallway and then frantically returned to Henry's arms. Henry told the girls to get the servants and call a doctor. Although his hands and face were burned, he thought only of his wife. She fainted and they carried her upstairs. The next day, Fanny Appleton Longfellow died.

Anne Longfellow Thorp confirmed this incident fifty-seven years after it happened and described it as related above. She said that she always thought it was her fault and blamed herself for her mother's death even though her father told her it was an accident.

The funeral was held only a few days later. It was July 13, 1861, which would have been their eighteenth wedding anniversary. Henry, whose face and hands were burned, was too injured to attend and his children stayed with relatives. Fanny was buried on the bluff plot, belonging to the Longfellows in Mount Auburn Cemetery in Cambridge.

What would Henry do now that the life of his beloved Fanny had ended too soon?

CHAPTER ELEVEN
"In the long, sleepless watches of the night"
Grief and Renewal

12. Longfellow and the family terrier, Trap.

Naturally, Henry felt empty and lost after the tragic passing of his wife. For days and weeks and months, he withdrew from everything. He couldn't write poetry or letters. He wouldn't go out to social events. His life was turned upside down and yet, he had to find a way to set it right; especially for his children.

Five weeks after Fanny's passing, he wrote a letter to her sister Mary in London and released his true feelings, "How I am alive after what my eyes have seen, I know not. I am at least patient, if not resigned, and thank God hourly—as I have from the beginning—for the beautiful life we led together, and that I loved her more and more to the end ... You can understand what an inexpressible delight she was to me, always and in all things. I never looked at her without a thrill of pleasure. She never came into a room where I was without my heart beating quicker, nor went out without my feeling that something of the light went with her. I loved her so entirely, and I know she was very happy."

Sadly, it took Henry eighteen years after Fanny's death to write about it on paper. On July 13, 1879, the eighteenth year after her passing, and their wedding anniversary day, Longfellow composed *The Cross of Snow*, while alone in his bedroom, staring at her portrait.

In the long, sleepless watches of the night,
*   A gentle face—the face of one long dead—*
*   Looks at me from the wall, where round its head*
The night-lamp casts a halo of pale light.

Here in this room she died; and soul more white
   Never through martyrdom of fire was led
   To its repose; nor can in books be read
   The legend of a life more benedight.
There is a mountain in the distant West
   That, sun-defying, in its deep ravines
   Displays a cross of snow upon its side.
Such is the cross I wear upon my breast
   These eighteen years, through all the changing scenes
   And seasons, changeless since the day she died.

After Fanny was gone from his life, many have commented on Henry's changed appearance. He grew a beard that flowed into his white mane of hair, which made him seem at least twenty years older. Some have said that the burns he sustained from Fanny's dress were the reason, but that myth has been dismissed.

There was only one place where Henry could go for comfort—Nahant. It was the perfect setting to restore his soul and give pleasure to his children to whom he never again mentioned the name of their mother. So, in August, the governess, servants, the children, and Henry retreated to their own cottage. Even Nahant brought back haunted memories of Fanny, but to him, they were happy ones.

Not only was Fanny's death a struggle for the children, but Fanny's father, Nathan Appleton, their beloved grandfather, had died within a few days of his daughter.

As a father, Henry had two active teenage sons, Charley (17) and Erny (15). Charley was wild and full of adventure. He had not the slightest interest in higher learning or in working for a bank in Boston. To his father's disappointment, Charley's dreams were about sailing and roaming the rocky cliffs and sandy beaches of Nahant and beyond. Perhaps Longfellow had forgotten that he, too, had stood at the edge of Casco Bay in Maine as a youth and dreamed of places across the Atlantic Ocean.

Longfellow's greatest fear was that Charley would run away to join the Army. Instead, he sailed with a friend of Longfellow's to an island near New Orleans, Louisiana, which was disease infested. Like a polished reporter, Charley wrote colorful details of everything he saw and heard. Next, Charley planned to go to Europe with a friend. Henry was in favor of his son's decision, but Charley really had another plan in mind.

It was hard to control Charley because he had inherited money from his mother and grandfather. He loved spending it!

Instead of going to Europe, Charley sent this letter to his father,

> Dear Papa,
> You know how long a time I have been wanting to go to war. I have tried hard to resist the temptation of going without your leave but I cannot any longer. I feel it to be my

first duty to do what I can for my country and I would willingly lay down my life for it if it would be of any good. God bless you all.

Yours affectionately,
Charley

Though Longfellow was in a constant state of worry, he may have understood that Charley probably had to prove that he was more than a famous man's son. After Charley joined a Massachusetts artillery division in Virginia in 1863, he was transferred to the Union cavalry in Washington, D.C.

As a single parent, Longfellow thought and prayed for his son in the heat of battle. When the Cambridge bells chimed in the distance on Christmas Day, he was inspired to write *Christmas Bells* as he longed for Charley to return safely home. Here is the last verse:

> *Then pealed the bells more loud and deep;*
> *"God is not dead; nor doth he sleep!*
> *The Wrong shall fail,*
> *The Right prevail,*
> *With peace on earth, good-will to men!"*

A Civil War battle resulted in a serious wound that brought his father to D.C. until Charley regained his strength to go home.

Once his children adjusted to new caregivers, Henry turned again to the production of poetry. In 1856, he had started work on something called *Tales of a Wayside Inn*. He pulled it from his files at the beginning of 1862 and resumed work on the 22 episodes of Part One.

Originally, Henry had used the title *Sudbury Tales*. Much later, he changed it to *Tales of a Wayside Inn*. The colonial-era Wayside Inn, once known as the Red-Horse Inn, still exists today as a popular restaurant and inn, located in Sudbury, Massachusetts. It was a house owned by Lyman Howe, who turned it into a stagecoach stop on route to and from Boston. Because of financial hardships, Howe was forced to convert his home into an inn. Here is an excerpt from *Tales of a Wayside Inn:*

> *One Autumn night, in Sudbury town,*
> *Across the meadows bare and brown,*
> *The windows of the wayside inn ...*

In constructing this large piece of work, Henry took his characters from real life and gave them different names. For example, Henry's friend, Luigi Monti, taught Italian at Harvard, but retreated to Sudbury in the summer to escape the city's humidity. Often Longfellow visited Luigi in Sudbury, and used him for his character, The Sicilian. The other characters were: The Innkeeper (Mr. Howe), The Student (Henry Ware Wales), The Theologian (Daniel Treadwell), The Poet (Thomas W. Parsons), and The Spanish Jew (Isaac Edrehi).

The Musician, Ole Bull—the famous virtuoso violinist from Norway—was a good friend of Longfellow and admired by Fanny. Ole Bull married Sara Thorp when she was twenty and he was sixty. Sara was Anne Allegra Longfellow Thorp's sister-in-law. Ole Bull and Sara lived in a villa in Norway that is now a museum. After his death, Sara built and lived in a house on Brattle Street in Cambridge.

Again, Longfellow hoped to stretch the minds of his readers beyond the North American borders to appreciate European cultures through *Tales of a Wayside Inn*. At the same time, the epic appreciated American culture as portrayed in *Paul Revere's Ride*.

> *You know the rest. In the books you have read,*
> *How the British Regulars fired and fled,—*
> *How the farmers gave them ball for ball,*
> *From behind each fence and farm-yard wall,*
> *Chasing the red-coats down the lane,*
> *Then, crossing the fields to emerge again*
> *Under the trees at the turn of the road,*
> *And only pausing to fire and load.*

While working on this long work, he was also researching and putting together *The New England Tragedies* about the witch trials. This wouldn't be published until 1868.

Other works included *Christus: A Mystery* (the story of Jesus) and *The Golden Legend* (about King Henry II and his romance). These poems did not appear until 1872.

The biggest project Longfellow undertook after Fanny's death was translating Dante's *Divine Comedy* from Italian into English. He started work on it in 1862, but it wasn't actually published until 1867.

America's history had its ups and downs in the late 1860s. It was still recovering from the Civil War and in the process of reuniting the North with the South. One of the biggest shocks to the nation was the assassination of President Abraham Lincoln in April of 1865. Between the aftermath of war and the loss of a president, the country was at a low point when Andrew Johnson succeeded Lincoln as president. Then in 1867, hope and optimism were renewed when the United States bought Alaska from Russia for $7 million dollars.

However, Henry's life took an upswing in 1865. He formed the Dante Club while translating *The Divine Comedy*. This was both a professional and social club that he assembled to help him with the perfect translation. They met weekly on Wednesday evenings to get together over dinner in his dining room and have long discussions afterwards—sometimes into the wee hours of the morning. When Longfellow mentioned the word "School-time," they would all pull their chairs around the table and listen to two cantos of his English translation. They would offer their suggestions and criticisms that Longfellow would ponder over the following week.

The two main members of the Dante Club were James Russell Lowell (poet and successor to Longfellow as the Professor of Modern Languages) and Charles Eliot Norton (American scholar). Some invited guests included Oliver Wendell Holmes (poet, author, and father of the future Supreme Court Justice), and William Dean Howells (journalist and editor). Henry's old terrier "Trap" attended every one of these gatherings—more for food than devotion to his master! One time he stole a partridge from the dinner table. The Dante Club became a model for the future Dante Society of America, which formed in 1881.

Meanwhile, Longfellow and his family continued to spend summers in Nahant with the occasional visit to Portland. His daughters especially liked to visit his sister Anne.

Charley and Erny were grown young men. They led their own lives. Finally, Charley went to Europe and traveled wherever he wanted. He seemed to be fond of Paris. Erny was drawn to mountain climbing and spent time in Conway, New Hampshire, hiking to the top of the White Mountains. However, both boys would return to Nahant, savoring the salt air. One summer Erny ventured to Europe and followed the journey his father had forged from 1826 to 1829. Inherited money made extensive travel possible.

Would Longfellow ever return to his beloved Europe?

Chapter Twelve

"Footprints on the sands of time"

Grand Tour and Final Years

13. Traveling in Venice in 1868 (left to right): Mary L. Greenleaf, Sam Longfellow, Alice Longfellow, H.W. Longfellow, Thomas Gold Appleton, Ernest Longfellow, Hattie Spellman Longfellow, Anne Pierce. Seated in front: Edith and Anne Longfellow.

Although Henry Longfellow enjoyed his busy life between Cambridge and Nahant, he had a desire to return to Europe again and introduce his large family to the places that meant so much to him as a young man.

That desire was fulfilled by a Grand Tour from June of 1868 to September of 1869. This time a party of eleven would accompany him, including his five children, his two sisters, Tom Appleton (Fanny's brother), Sam Longfellow (his brother), Erny's bride Hattie, and Miss Davie, a former governess to the Longfellow children.

Throughout Great Britain and Continental Europe, the big group went sightseeing while Henry was the center of attention everywhere they went because of his extraordinary fame and accomplishments. Everyone of note wanted to entertain him. There were honorary degrees bestowed on him at Oxford and Cambridge.

Wherever the Longfellow clan went, they were received with respect. Henry met and dined with politicians, royalty, and other recognized poets in Great Britain, such as Alfred, Lord Tennyson.

Perhaps the most honored invitation came from Queen Victoria, who requested Longfellow visit her at Windsor Castle. She was astounded by his breadth of knowledge and his prolific output of poetry. It was she who was impressed by his presence along with her servants, who lined the corridor of the castle as he exited. Many of them could recite his poems by heart. To them, Longfellow was royalty—a King of Poetry.

While the travelers were in Rome, the Hungarian composer/pianist, Franz Liszt, insisted on giving a concert in Longfellow's honor. He had set The Prologue from Longfellow's *The Golden Legend* to music. The portrait artist George P.A. Healy painted Longfellow and his daughter Edith from a photograph as well as a portrait of Liszt (thanks to Longfellow's introduction of the two men). In her Rome Studio, African-American sculptor Edmondia Lewis made a marble bust of Longfellow, which is now in Harvard's collection. The famed British photographer Julia Margaret Cameron, took one of the most famous photographs of Longfellow on the Isle of Wight. He was posed in profile with his snowy beard and hair, which reminded people of Shakespeare's character, King Lear.

Back in America, Longfellow continued to produce poetry. *Tales of a Wayside Inn* went into a second series in 1870 and three *Books of Song* were printed two years later. In 1874, the history of poetry appeared in 31 volumes as *Poems and Places*. From 1875 to 1882, and even after his death, more sonnets were published. Many were commentaries of political events set into verse.

In the year 1875, Bowdoin President Joshua Chamberlain asked Longfellow to speak at the 50th reunion of his 1825 class. It was to be given at the sturdy, gray First Parish Congregational Church with its square tower that stands guard outside the gates of Bowdoin today. Inside are the wooden Gothic arches and straight wooden pews that hosted such greats as Harriet Beecher Stowe and in more recent times, Martin Luther King, Jr. With strong conviction, their messages of unity and social reform were heard by the congregation.

For the occasion, Longfellow wrote a special poem, *Morituri Salutamus* (We salute the dead). It was a tribute to scholars, both ancient and modern.

> *The scholar and the world! The endless strife,*
> *The discord in the harmonies of life!*
> *The love of learning, the sequestered nooks,*
> *And all the serenity of books;*
> *The market-place, the eager love of gain,*
> *Whose aim is vanity, and whose end is pain!*

However, the words Henry delivered from the pulpit could hardly be heard. He was still a shy man when it came to public speaking.

Henry's family gave him comfort throughout his life. None of them became writers, although his brother, Samuel Longfellow, a minister, wrote many hymns still sung today, assembled Henry's correspondence into published volumes, and wrote his biography.

Charley never really had a job, but continued his adventures in the Orient. He lived in Japan from 1871 to 1873, spending much of his fortune on treasured artifacts. While there, he had his body tattooed before such a daring thing was accepted. An entire room on the second floor of Craigie House was called the Japan Room, wallpapered in an oriental theme with fans. Erny became a professional artist and patron of the arts. He donated many paintings, including his own work, to the Museum of Fine Arts in Boston. He also painted a portrait of his father in oil, which still rests on an easel in Longfellow's study. Both Edith and Anne married, and Alice, who never married, became keeper and historic protector of the Craigie House throughout her lifetime. She helped co-found Radcliffe College, which was the female counterpart of Harvard College until the two institutions merged.

When the house became empty-nested, Longfellow followed the advice of Professor Ticknor, given decades before, to continue intellectual labor in the face of difficult times and loneliness.

As the aging years continued, Henry wrote something called, *Michael Angelo: a Fragment.* Longfellow must have been remembering his early years in Rome and thinking about Michelanglo's life and his production of art for the Medici family.

> *How will men speak of me when I am gone,*
> *When all this colorless, sad life is ended,*
> *And I am as dust? They will remember only*
> *The wrinkled forehead, the marred countenance,*
> *The rudeness of my speech, and my rough manners,*
> *And never dream that underneath them all*
> *There was a woman's breast of tenderness;*
> *They will not know the secret of my life,*

Locked up in silence, or but vaguely hinted
In uncouth rhymes, that may perchance survive
Some little space in memories of men!

Surely Longfellow was writing about himself, too.

In his later years, Longfellow was a celebrity in America and Europe. His house on Brattle Street was the center for famous visitors to come pay their respects, but also for ordinary people, who knocked on the large front door of his yellow house, hoping to glimpse the famous poet. He welcomed one and all. Native Americans came. Heads of State came. Famous actresses came. Some curiosity seekers even peeked in the windows, but wouldn't come inside.

As always, Henry adored children and welcomed them to the house. In 1879, the children of Cambridge presented him with a birthday gift. It was an armchair made out of the "spreading chestnut-tree" that he had written about in *The Village Blacksmith*. Against Longfellow's wishes and objections from others, chestnut trees were cut down to widen Brattle Street. Despite his regret over this, he received the gift with great joy. Longfellow wrote a poem *From My Arm-chair*, thanking the children for their gift and giving them a copy when they visited the house.

Am I a king, that I should call my own
This splendid ebon throne?
Or by what reason, or what right divine,
Can I proclaim it mine?

Some of Longfellow's famous phrases are quoted and spoken in everyday conversation by a public that rarely realizes that Longfellow is the originator. Here are a few:

Ships that pass in the night

One if by land, and two if by sea

Between the dark and the daylight

The patter of little feet

This is the forest primeval

The wreck of the Hesperus

Two of Longfellow's great qualities were loyalty and generosity to his friends. George W. Greene, whom he had met in Rome during his first trip to Europe, was a recipient of these gestures. Greene returned from Rome in poor health and stayed in Craigie House while he recovered. Henry even paid to have Greene's writing published. Somehow Greene had never succeeded in the literary world.

On March 24, 1882, Henry Wadsworth Longfellow died in his home with his family around him. He would join his two wives in the plot at Mount Auburn Cemetery.

Although interest in Longfellow's work—particularly in New England—continues, national enthusiasm has faded. Some scholars pinpoint two world wars; others blame greater industrialization, technology, and television, which have diminished a reverence for the written word. Third, school curriculums have given a backseat to American History and Literature.

According to poet-critic J. D. McClatchy, modern poets such as W.H. Auden, Ezra Pound, and T.S. Eliot made fun of Longfellow for his elegant, delicate, and moralizing style. Rhymes and meters were laughed at while free verse became the best friend of 20th century poets. Poet Robert Frost, however, was the exception. Frost had great respect for Longfellow and delighted in his rhythm of rhyme and meter as Shakespeare had used centuries before in his sonnets.

Despite the ebb and flow of poetic trends, Henry Wadsworth Longfellow will always be part of the global literary landscape. He is the only American to have a marble bust in the Poets' Corner of Westminster Abbey in London. It has been there since 1884.

The Bicentennial celebration in 2007 has renewed a nostalgic interest in the works of Longfellow, who was called the "poet of the people." In the English-speaking world, his works were widely read and memorized by mill workers and royalty. Generations of children learned to read and enjoy Longfellow's poetry. In fact, his lasting influence can be seen in the use of his name on hundreds of schools, libraries, streets, and public buildings. Even the architectural design of his home in Cambridge was copied and reproduced across the country.

Today, the Longfellow House on Brattle Street in Cambridge is a National Historic Site, which houses 750,000 papers that include 600 papers from the period George Washington lived in the house. There are toys that belonged to the Longfellow children as well as costumes and other clothing. Many of these documents, books, and pieces from history are in the archives in the basement of the Longfellow House. Other papers can be found at Harvard's Houghton Library, Bowdoin College, and the Maine Historical Society. The furnished rooms and art throughout the Longfellow House remain as they were from 1843 to 1882. Longfellow's childhood home in Portland, Maine, is maintained by the Maine Historical Society.

Because of Longfellow's travels to Europe, he was considered "a citizen of the world." He introduced Americans to literature from other countries and commanded respect from many nations.

The modern word "multi-culturalist" has been attached to Longfellow because of his sensitivity to the trials and traditions of Blacks and American Indians in his epic poems. Furthermore, his role as "storyteller" created a national identity for Americans through his poetic portrayals of historic events and figures such as Paul Revere, Miles Standish, Hiawatha, and Evangeline.

In conclusion, Henry Wadsworth Longfellow's life and works remain in the "memories of men." His poetry still speaks to the lives and souls of people, regardless of the century.

Timeline

1805   Brother Stephen Longfellow is born.

1807   Born February 27 in Portland, ME.

1808   Sister Elizabeth is born.

1810   Sister Anne is born.

1813   Starts at Portland Academy.

1814   Brother Alexander is born.

1816   Sister Mary is born.

1818   Sister Ellen is born.

1819   Brother Samuel is born.

1820   First poem is published.

1821   Enrolled at Bowdoin College in Brunswick, ME.

1826   Sails for France in April for a three-year study of European languages and cultures.

1829   Begins teaching at Bowdoin College.

1831   Marries Mary Storer Potter of Portland.

1835   *Outre Mer* is published. Sails for Europe with Mary. Mary dies November 29.

1837   Forms "The Five of Clubs" while teaching at Harvard. Rents rooms in Craigie House in Cambridge.

1842   Publishes poems on slavery in November.

1843   Marries Fanny Appleton, July 13. They live at Craigie House.

1844   Son Charles Appleton is born June 9.

1845   Son Ernest Wadsworth is born November 23.

1847   *Evangeline* is published November 1.

1850   Daughter Alice Mary is born September 22.

1853   Daughter Edith is born October 22.

1854	Resigns from Harvard February 16.
1855	Daughter Anne Allegra is born November 8. *The Song of Hiawatha* is published June 25.
1858	*The Courtship of Miles Standish* is published October 16.
1861–63	Fanny dies July 10, 1861. *Tales of a Wayside Inn* published in November 1863. Charles runs away to join the army.
1868	Son Erny marries Harriet Spelman May 21. Sails to Europe with family for a Grand Tour.
1878	Daughter Edith marries Richard Henry Dana, III, January 10.
1879	For his birthday, the children of Cambridge give him an armchair, made from the chestnut tree, mentioned in *The Village Blacksmith*.
1882	Dies March 24 and is buried at Mount Auburn Cemetery in Cambridge.

Questions for Discussion

1. Longfellow's childhood in Portland, Maine, gave him lifelong memories of the picturesque New England town and its seafaring lifestyle. How did the Wadsworth and Longfellow families influence him? Did they support his writing interests?

2. How did Longfellow react to the news of the Trustees of Bowdoin College appointing him Instructor at a reduced salary instead of Professor of Modern Languages? Did his father approve of his action?

3. Longfellow learned to speak eight languages and read twelve. What countries did he visit in Europe during his four visits abroad? Besides talking with people, how did the wandering scholar become so fluent?

4. Many different people helped Longfellow during his lifetime. Who were his contemporaries and role models? What similarities and differences are there among all these people? How was he a leader like his hero Washington?

5. Discuss Longfellow's attitude towards slavery. How was he ahead of his times? In what other ways was he a cultural force?

6. In 1819 W.C. Bryant wrote a popular poem about death. In 1838 Longfellow broke the gloomy mood of the era and wrote an optimistic poem, *A Psalm of Life, What the Heart of the Young Man Said to the Psalmist*. Why would Longfellow write such a poem when he himself faced grief and loss?

7. Discuss other topics mentioned in this book such as, The American Revolution, the Victorian age, the U.S. Civil War, Native Americans, and other authors of the period.

8. Longfellow, the American genius, used his extraordinary literary talents to encourage understanding of different cultures. There is a genius in us all. What are your talents?

9. Longfellow was the most widely read American poet in the English speaking world for almost 100 years. Why did he appeal to every class, from mill workers to royalty? What parallels does his work have in today's world?

10. What icons in American history are found in Longfellow's poems?

Places to Visit and Web Sites

The Wadsworth-Longfellow House
485 Congress Street
Portland, ME 04101
The author's beloved childhood home, a brick Federal style house, was built by Longfellow's grandfather, General Peleg Wadsworth, after the Revolutionary War.
www.mainehistory.org
Phone: 207-774-1822

Longfellow House-Washington's Headquarters
National Historic Site
105 Brattle Street
Cambridge, MA 02138
The Longfellows' Georgian style home of 45 years was a wedding present in 1843 from his father-in-law, Nathan Appleton. General George Washington used the house as his headquarters during the Siege of Boston.
www.nps.gov/long
Phone: 617-876-4491

Longfellow's Wayside Inn
Route 20
Sudbury, MA 01776
Longfellow's Wayside Inn, established in 1716, inspired the poet's popular poem, *Tales of a Wayside Inn* which includes *Paul's Revere's Ride*.
www.wayside.org
Phone: 978-443-1776

Old North Church
193 Salem Street
Boston, MA 02113
Longfellow memorialized the historic Old North Church in one of his most famous poems, *Paul Revere's Ride*.
Open every day to the public with tours and a gift shop.
www.oldnorth.com
Phone: 617-523-6676

Plimoth Plantation
137 Warren Avenue
Plymouth, MA 02360
"Living Breathing History" comes alive at Plimoth on a seasonal basis. Longfellow chose the pilgrims, Priscilla Mullins and John Alden, to tell about a romantic love triangle in *The Courtship of Miles Standish*.
www.plimoth.org
Phone: 508-746-1622

Pilgrim Hall Museum
75 Court Street
Plymouth, MA 02360

"The possessions and artifacts of the Pilgrims tell the story of brave and determined men and women, and their attempts to build lives and homes for themselves and their children in a new world." See John Alden's Bible, cupboard, and sword.

www.pilgrimhall.org
Phone: 508-746-1620

St. Martinville Tourist Information Center
125 South New Market Street
St. Martinville, LA 70582

The attractions in St. Martinville tell the tale of the French-speaking people of the Bayou Teche area and Longfellow's legend of the ill-fated lovers, Evangeline and Gabriel. The area includes the Acadian Memorial, St. Martinville Cultural Heritage Center, Evangeline Monument and more.

www.stmartinville.org
Phone: 337-394-2233

Grand Pre' National Historic Site of Canada
2205 Grand Pre' Road
Grand Pre', Nova Scotia BOP 1MO
Canada

This is the site of the church and cemetery of the 17th–18th century village that burned during the tragic expulsion of

the Acadians. Longfellow used the setting in his narrative poem, *Evangeline*. The Visitor Centre includes multimedia presentations on the Acadians. Nearby is the Statue of Evangeline.
www.grand-pre.com
Phone: 1-866-452-3631

Bibliography

1. Aaron, Daniel; Butler, Joyce. *Longfellow's Portland and Portland's Longfellow*. Maine Historical Society. 1987.

2. Butler, Joyce; D'Abate, Richard; Sprague, Laura Fecych. *Henry Wadsworth Longfellow and His Portland Home*. Maine Historical Society. 2004.

3. Calhoun, Charles C. *Longfellow, A Rediscovered Life*. Beacon Press, Boston. 2004.

4. Canby, Henry Seidel. *Favorite Poems of Henry Wadsworth Longfellow*. Doubleday and Co., New York. 1947.

5. Harberts, Ethel F. *An American Bard. The Story of Henry W. Longfellow*. Versa Press, East Peoria, Illinois. 1993.

6. Hilen, Andrew (editor). *The Letters of Henry Wadsworth Longfellow. Volumes I-IV.* Belknap Press of Harvard University Press, Cambridge, Massachusetts, 1972.

7. Irmscher, Christoph. *Longfellow Redux*. University of Illinois Press, Champaign, Illinois. 2006.

8. Longfellow National Historic Site. *Footprints on the Sands of Time*. Eastern National Park and Monument Association. 1996.

9. Longfellow, Samuel (editor). Three volumes. Volume I. *The Life of Henry Wadsworth Longfellow*. Houghton

Mifflin and Company, Boston and New York; 1891, 1968.

10. Patterson, Stanley C.; Seaburg, Carl G. *Nahant on the Rocks.* Nahant Historical Society. 1991.

11. Wagenknecht, Edward. *Henry Wadsworth Longfellow, Portrait of an American Humanist.* Oxford University Press, New York, 1966.

12. Wagenknecht, Edward (editor). *Mrs. Longfellow: Selected Letters and Journals of Fanny Appleton Longfellow (1817–1861).* Longmans, Green, and Co. New York, London, Toronto. 1956.

About the Authors

MARIAN (HANNAH) CARLSON is a writer and educator. She published over 100 articles as a syndicated columnist for an international daily newspaper. As a literature and writing teacher for over 15 years, more than 50 of her students have been published in national chlidren's magazines. As a writing teacher in Lexington and Brookline, her programs for middle school students received special recognition from the Harvard Graduate School of Education. Hannah has received grants from the National Endowment for the Arts, PBS and others to write educational programs. See www.hwlongfellow.org/teachers for information about lesson plans on Longfellow and the Forging of American Identity. Her other recent books are *John Adams: The Voice Heard 'Round the World* and *In Search of the Great American Writers.* As co-chair of the Longfellow Bicentennial Committee, Hannah was instrumental in obtaining the Longfellow postage stamp and in organizing many celebrations of Longfellow's 200th birthday, including Longfellow's Gala at Harvard University's Sanders Theatre. Her book on John Adams was put to music and recorded by the Boston Landmarks Orchestra in a companion CD narrated by Pulitzer Prize winner David McCullough. This book and CD set was honored as a Parents' Choice Gold Award Winner in 2011. The John Adams book won the New England Book Show Award, Best in Category Elem-High School in 2012. In addition to her writing, Hannah is very active with homeschooling. She lives with her family in Cambridge overlooking Longfellow Park.

The late LIBBY HUGHES was an author, award-winning playwright and lyricist. She edited Ginger Rogers' autobiography and won the Maxwell Anderson Playwrights Series in 1984. Several of her plays have been produced off Broadway. Of her sixteen books, she has written twelve biographies for young adults.

978-0-984-47763-0
0-984-47763-2